WAYFINDING

Navigating Your Personal Evolution and
Professional Growth Mountains

Christy Uffelman, MHCS, BCC

SB
PRESS

To Kevin, my anchor

To Eli, my wings

*To Dr. Mary Shippy, my Wayfinding
Mountain Guide*

CONTENTS

Foreword.. 1

Introduction: Hitting the Trail................................. 5

CHAPTER 1: The Wayfinding Journey........................ 9
Field, Forest, and Summit

CHAPTER 2: The Wayfinding Compass...................... 26
Building Your Personal Evolution Model

CHAPTER 3: Self-Awareness................................. 46
Finding Your True North

CHAPTER 4: Self-Alignment................................. 60
Building Your Vitality Voltage

CHAPTER 5: Self-Trust.....................................78
Befriending Your Inner Critic

CHAPTER 6: Self-Worth.....................................94
Reprogramming Your Belief Systems

CHAPTER 7: Don't Go It Alone.............................109
The Value of Third Places and Peer Groups

CHAPTER 8: Your Companions...............................140
The Three Wayfinding Mountain Guides

CHAPTER 9: You Have Your Compass and
Your Mountain Guides—Now What?...............................160

Afterword: Mapmaking—It's Your Time to Climb...............171

Endnotes 174

FOREWORD

She stood up abruptly, the conference room chair rolling back from behind her knees. She firmly placed both palms flat on the table in front of me, eagerly leaned forward, and nearly shouted, "You are going to change the world!"

I was twenty-four years old. We were in a basement meeting room—no windows, fluorescent lighting, and the elevator mechanical room humming behind us. The nonverbals were a stark contrast to Christy's pleated skirt and tweed blazer, but one thing was certain: I believed her.

This was the first time I had ever met Christy Uffelman, and over the next fifteen plus years I would bear witness to the gift and the hard work that developed into that magic inside of her. Long before I developed my own language for what I have learned both personally and professionally alongside Christy, it was very clear that whatever it was, it came from *inside* and not *outside* a person.

As a human resources executive for public and private companies, I have spent twenty years researching, developing, strategizing, and frankly trying to understand human potential. After all that time, what if I told you that most of what the world, social media, or corporate frameworks lead you to believe about your own potential is just plain wrong? What if the *idea* of potential itself could be the limiting factor?

Potential. We have all heard it; we have all said it.

"She has a ton of potential. She's just naturally gifted."

"He never had the potential to succeed anyway."

"We want to invest in our high potentials at this company."

Okay, then, what the hell is potential?

I could easily rattle off ten different textbook definitions to answer that question, but the reality is that for all the reasons you are reading this book—Potential. Does. Not. Matter.

But you know what does? Momentum.

And this book is going to teach you how to build it—from the inside out.

Whether we have taken the time to think about it or not, we are all constantly evaluating our own personal potential. We consciously and unconsciously put it in the driver's seat when we set goals, apply for jobs, join a gym, or consider a romantic partner. We hold up the measuring stick to our future selves before we even begin. And then sometimes we choose not to begin at all.

But momentum, oh momentum, it does not discriminate. Momentum naturally assumes that every person can build it. You see, where potential judges you based on the past, your environment, or some other factor outside yourself, momentum is simply you from the inside choosing forward motion. No matter how big or how small that forward motion is, anyone and everyone can make progress.

Think of momentum like a locomotive getting started. It can take a lot of energy and effort to get the wheels to move around once, but the next rotation gets a bit easier and a bit faster. Eventually, you are flying down the tracks, and the curve in the road or the uphill grade that would have grinded you to a halt at the beginning is barely on your radar anymore.

If you choose, this book can be the first step to your own momentum. As you learn and explore the importance of the Wayfinding Compass and its cardinal directions of Self-Awareness, Self-Alignment, Self-Trust, and ultimately Self-Worth, Christy will help you break through the noise that comes from inside of you and tap into the boundless momentum you can build through the person you have always been.

And let us not forget, the power in all of us starts from within, and we always find company beside us along the way. Those peer companions keep our heads up when our chins drop, challenge us when we doubt our authenticity, and hold us accountable to show up for ourselves and our goals when we waver.

As you will read on the pages that follow, that companionship and community become what Ray Oldenburg defined in his 1989 book *The Great Good Place* as a **Third Place**—a space that falls outside our home life and our work life that serves a primary purpose of connection and belonging. Most of our Third Places took a big hit during the pandemic. Some dissolved, some had to pivot their purpose, and others shuttered their doors completely. Layer that on top of an increasingly digital social landscape, and many of us find ourselves absent the proverbial compass we once took for granted. Now more than ever in most of our lifetimes we need to learn how to create and sustain our own Third Places. This Field Guide will direct you to find (or create) your own peer group that will keep your momentum moving and nurture those critically vulnerable and consistent spaces that help us connect and belong.

At twenty-five years old, I did not have this book to help put words around the profound experience I was living shortly after

I met Christy Uffelman the first time. After just one year of self-reflection, conversation, and companionship around this model of personal evolution, I had the realization that **the world was not coming at me, but I was coming at the world**. That audacious declaration from my first meeting with Christy becomes more of a reality each day. And I have no doubt that your Wayfinding journey with her through this book will do the same for you.

May you all leave your mark on this world.

MICHELLE BUCZKOWSKI,
CHRO, Eos Energy

INTRODUCTION
Hitting the Trail

I t is time. You know it. And I know it. It is a time of great suffering and a time of great promise.

The meaning you find behind those words is in what you just chose to read in that sentence. What resonated with you?

A time of great suffering—did you think of the terrifying and truly awful atrocities in our world right now? The divisiveness? The mental health crisis? The epidemic of loneliness?

Or did you hear that it is a time of great promise? After all, every beginning needs an ending to happen first. What if we are living in a time of powerful disruptions to old, outdated patterns? Of aligning human wisdom beside AI? Of breaking down to break through? Of hope?

Some folks will be drawn to one extreme or the other. Lately I have been on both sides on the same day, sometimes even in the same hour.

Research would tell you that the Meaning-Making Machine that lives inside our heads—the human brain—is hardwired to find patterns, wired to grasp for control to mitigate fear. In my work as a coach for nearly thirty years, I have learned that a big part of being human is about having an acute awareness of this fact and evolving past it. We must understand instead that we can challenge the status quo of our thinking (and feeling) to realize our personal power to choose our next step forward with intention—to Wayfind, to fully realize the magnitude of the reality that we are not the *actor* in our stories but the *author of them*. Or as Michelle said so eloquently in the Foreword, it is to recognize for the first time, maybe ever, that the world is not coming at me but that I am coming at the world.

Consider me right now at this moment. I am under a code red/final-Final-*Final* deadline (this book in your hands should have been published eighteen months ago), feeling like I have so much to say and yet writing nothing. I procrastinate. I fear. Why? Because my mind has written a story that I am not good enough to reach those who need this personal evolution model right now. I can hear my Inner Critic voice—strong, loud, and clear. It says there is still more research to do before publication. It says the world isn't ready for this work, and neither are you.

And I believe it.

Because the story I write in my head is true, right?

But what if there was an alternative to my brain's approach? How about my soul? Since *soul* is one of those words that folks may find divisive, let's instead refer to it as our gut. For me, I call this counterbalance to my head my deep Belly Wisdom— where my truth and intuition live. You see, when I give myself permission to quiet my fearful brain and drop down through my body, listening through my heart and my emotions and then down again, even deeper down into my Belly, I can hear a very different voice—softer, slower. This voice does not need to yell. In fact, it is barely above a whisper most days. I must be grounded and still in my body and my spirit to even hear it. But when I stop and ask, "Is it time?"

The answer is *yes*.

And so we will begin.

1

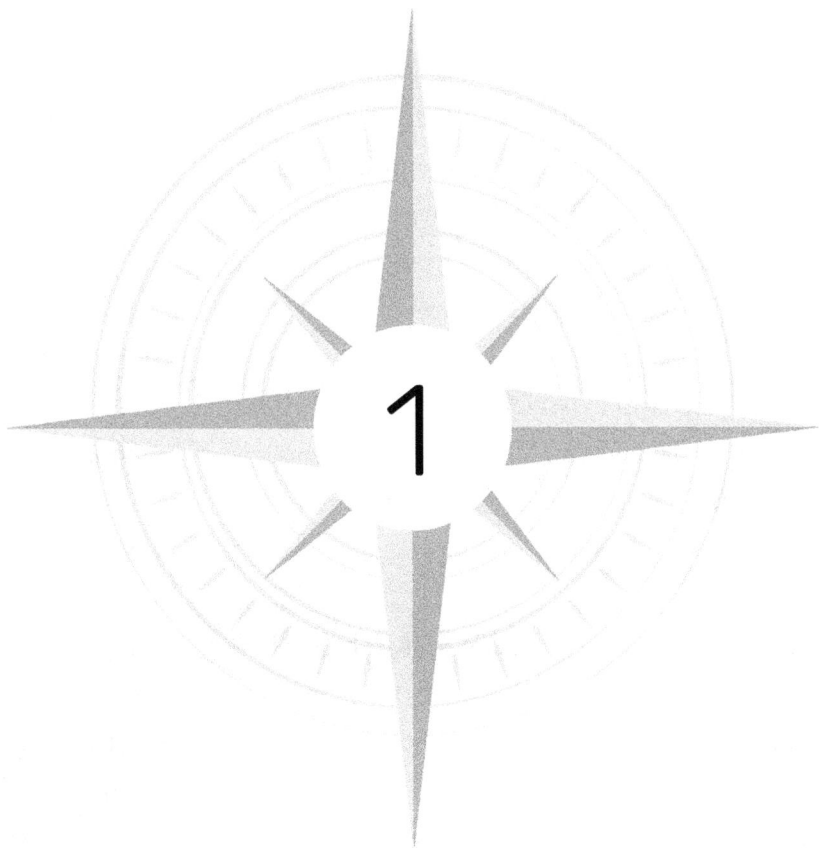

THE WAYFINDING JOURNEY
Field, Forest, and Summit

I am quite a reluctant expert on personal evolution. Through a series of terrible choices in both my personal and professional life in my twenties and thirties, and more than a few since, I discovered the power of human transformation and reinvention out of sheer desperation to save myself—or to use the concept of Belly Wisdom, to lead myself.

I have spent twenty-five years in the leadership development space, and the competency least studied, taught, and talked about is the skill of leading yourself. It spans the gender spectrum, race and ethnicity, culture, orientation, and generation. Leading yourself authentically requires personal accountability. Agency. It's what I like to call radical self-responsibility. And when done well, its gift is an authentic and aligned life.

It is what led me to shift my focus and ultimately my company from leadership to personal development. It is understanding that we are whole people. What happens at work comes home with me every day. And you'd better believe that what is cooking for me at home shows up at work. I believe we need to grow the person to grow the leader.

What I learned in my research in the space of personal development is that the sum of the experience is greater than its parts. My own personal development, or what I refer to as my Wayfinding journey, is the result of personal mentorship from well-known global thought leaders such as Brené Brown and quiet gurus in spaces you may have never heard of, and especially from accompanying more than 12,000 leaders globally on their journeys over the last twelve years. Said differently, I am more than all I have been. And I will become more than I am now.

The journey of personal evolution is being able to identify and fully access at will your own personal power. And this skill is needed more now than maybe ever before in our lifetimes, given where the world is economically and geopolitically. We know that what happens at the macro happens at the micro, and in that way, perhaps personal evolution is the most powerful action we can all take to change the world in this moment and for the future. When I have unfettered access to my personal power, I no longer need to fight to achieve situational power. When I treat myself with respect, compassion, and care, I no longer need to please, perfect, prove, or perform to gain them from others.

As humans, we can only treat people as well as we treat ourselves. If I hold myself to unrealistic expectations, I will show up as a taskmaster at work. If I feel inadequate as a parent, I will become a never-satisfied mother. Said in another way, if I don't truly and genuinely like myself, no one else in turn will simply ever be good enough. The impact of this internal schism ripples across the domains of where I am in life as a boss, a teammate, a partner, a parent, and of course, a citizen of the world.

The words that follow on the pages to come are not mine alone, and I will never take credit for them as the originator. No idea in this book is unique to me. My evolving work rests on the ideas of many masters, both contemporary and ancient. From Rumi to Carl Jung. From Bessel Van der Kolk to Najwa Zebian. From Buddha to Byron Katie. We all share the same story; we only tell it in different ways to different audiences. My audience of choice is in the workplace—corporations, executives, leaders, everyday folks like you. I meet people where we all spend the majority of our waking hours—at work.

Wayfinding is an ancient art of mapmaking. The path toward personal evolution works less like a GPS where you can plug in your desired destination and get turn-by-turn directions, and more like the explorers of old. Wayfinding is building your map as you go. And no one builds maps of new lands alone.

While the *what* behind each Wayfinding journey is different from person to person, the *how*, the process itself, is as old as the stars that guide it. According to Caroline Myss's model, personal evolution happens first through the steps of revolution (I must break down to break through), involution (going inward to assess what tools and gifts I have access to), and evolution (trying new behaviors on for size, failing, and trying again). It is building your leadership and life skill of developing personal consciousness—the ability to release the old to embrace the new, with the awareness that all things end at the appropriate time and begin at the appropriate time.

Wayfinding is living fully in the present moment as you keep moving, knowing that no person or situation will be exactly the same tomorrow. Wayfinding is flow.

We lead, we evolve, we transform, and we heal through four aspects that each supports, buttresses, and deepens the others.

- **Self-Awareness:** The *what*—understanding who you truly are, what drives you, what you truly want, and where you excel.

- **Self-Alignment:** The *how*—aligning your actions, values, and goals with intentional rest and recovery cycles so you harness the energy needed to move forward with confidence and clarity.

- **Self-Trust:** The *when*—building the courage to trust your instincts, befriend your Inner Critic, set and sustain boundaries to make bold decisions that matter, practice self-compassion, take risks, and stay loyal to yourself at all costs.

- **Self-Worth:** The *who*—recognizing the value you bring to the table and how that impacts your self-view as much as it does your relationships with family, friends, and organizations, and intentionally reprogramming your belief system.

Like brave and bold explorers across every continent, humans were not meant to travel alone. We have been built to evolve in relationships with others. And yet somehow, knowing this truth deep in our Belly, it often brings fear instead of hope. As humans, we have a limiting belief system that if I don't [fill in the blank here], you will leave me. Many of us thus focus on pleasing the other in the attempt to protect ourselves from being alone, believing that if I can perform in the ways you want me to, if I can show up as perfect, then you will not leave me. And so we are conditioned to self-abandon.

In a world that feels increasingly volatile—from politics to climate change, from AI to mental health—it is understandable that self-repression feels like a safe place for many of us. And this is the exact path that slowly led me to crippling anxiety and deep depression. I can promise you that while numbing out and avoiding feeling familiar, it is not safe, my friends.

As humans, staying in our comfort zone rarely serves us. Our Wayfinding journey toward personal evolution is recognizing that right now—at this exact moment—we already have all we need. You have come to this place with all the knowledge already deep inside you—in your Head, your Heart, and your Belly.[1] Personal evolution is less of learning and more of remembering.

In fact, the Wayfinding Compass is already in your pocket. The task now at hand is to learn how to use it. And if you find that you have gotten off course, as happens often when we journey to new lands, you will know exactly how to calibrate it when needed with the help of three powerful Mountain Guides.

This book is my vulnerable journey through my own personal evolution (so far, anyway), knowing that, as you will soon learn,

Wayfinding is never about personal mastery. That's because we never "arrive," or as the old saying goes, the destination is never the goal. *The journey itself is the goal.* I am sharing my story with you in the hope that you will see yourself not only in my practice but in my failures. As we live life fully as humans, we *will* fall, and we will break. And it is when we break that we can finally see all the parts of us we needed to see all along.

We cannot just try to fix ourselves like we're putting together broken pieces of pottery. Instead, we must reconstruct, which means becoming aware. "Unbreaking," according to Najwa Zebian in her book *Welcome Home*, "mean[s] wishing the pain away. And that is impossible."[2]

Personal evolution is the messiest and the most beautiful form of unraveling. If you doubt me, here is how you will know it is right. As you read the pages of this Wayfinding Field Guide of sorts, something—maybe even only a single line—will resonate with you as truth. You will know it when you feel it—deep in your Belly. Truth doesn't need facts to prove it is truth. Truth is not a doing or even a feeling; it is a knowing. Maybe it has already happened. And when that moment hits, I invite you to keep reading. Excavate these nuggets of truth as key mile markers for your Wayfinding journey.

Throughout the book I offer you space to reflect and capture your own Field Notes. That is the exquisite beauty of being human, that no one person's evolution is exactly the same and yet the process is identical. The Wayfinding experience is individual, but the process of evolution is collective.

DISCOVERING GROWTH MOUNTAINS

I will never forget my first big professional failure. I had just graduated from college. I was recruited by Johnson & Johnson to sell surgical equipment for their medical device division called Ethicon Endo-Surgery, Inc.

It was at a time when medical instrumentation and surgical equipment sales were at their height, and everybody wanted to get into it. With my part-time sales experience while I was in college and graduating in three years instead of four, I had a leg up on my same-age competitors for the job. I thought I had hit the lottery. There I was, at the ripe age of twenty-one, out there thinking, *I've got this!* I had a big-time job with a big-name company paycheck to go along with it.

I hit the ground running. I naturally gravitate toward people and creating connections, and Johnson & Johnson had a robust training program for recent college grads, so I was able to be a pretty decent salesperson right off the bat. And because I was good at what I was doing, after a couple of years, my results were noticed by my boss and my boss's boss. I was selected to be part of a company-wide mentoring program designed for high-potential young leaders.

This was back in the early 2000s before companies and coaches knew what we know now. It was a very formal, very traditional mentoring program where I was assigned a mentor almost like it was an arranged marriage. Good sales reps mentored new hires, and good sales managers mentored good reps—all the way up to the C-suite.

Even though my mentor and I never really clicked, as often happens in programs like this, I fell in love with adult learning and development. Of course, at the time I didn't even have the language for this thing I was becoming so passionate about. All I knew was that the time I spent mentoring new hires was incredibly fulfilling in a way that meeting my sales quota was not.

I enjoyed talking with new sales reps about what their goals were, how they were going to achieve them, and of course, how I could best support them as a companion and accountability partner. It was incredibly fun helping them establish credibility and visibility, not only with their clients but with their peers, manager, and team.

Given my youth and inexperience, I quite naively assumed that this must be what management was all about, that being a manager of people was primarily about developing those people to become their best selves. And since I had enough Self-Awareness to know that I loved developing people *way more* than I loved hitting my own sales goal (shocker), I assumed the next step in my career trajectory was that I should be a sales manager. So I started looking into how I could get a promotion to the sales manager role within the company.

At the time, Johnson & Johnson didn't promote sales team members to managers within the same territory to avoid people managing their former peers. If you wanted to move up within the organization, you had to physically move, which for me meant leaving my hometown of Pittsburgh.

As a young single mom at the time, moving away from my family and my support system was a nonstarter. So instead, I went through a recruiting firm and landed at Bayer, another global healthcare organization, this time selling capital diagnostic equipment to hospitals. It kept me in the realm of sales and still in healthcare, but this time, I was a sales manager.

And it didn't even take me a year to go down in flames.

It quickly became clear to me that the qualities that make someone an A+ salesperson (which I wasn't, but let's just say I was) don't necessarily make them an A+ manager. In fact, an A+ salesperson will more likely be a rather poor sales manager because being a good people manager requires a totally different skill set than a salesperson.

In my case, I found that I couldn't hold anyone accountable for results. I just wanted everyone to like me. It got to the point that I was actually doing my people's jobs for them, mostly because it was the only way I could guarantee the high-level outcomes I was used to achieving. I disengaged my people, depleted my energy, and started to burn out.

Luckily for me, Bayer didn't fire me, although they absolutely could have and likely should have. Instead, they pipelined me into Learning and Organization Development. That is where I first encountered the field of coaching.

Like a cartoon revelation, the skies parted, the sun came out, and the light bulb above my head blinked on. I was so astonished to realize there was a job that was purely focused on developing people, and it was called *coaching*.

I share this story to introduce you to my first experience with what I have since come to call Growth Mountains. In the twenty-five years since, I have used this critical component for personal and professional development with our clients at EDGE Leadership. In fact, in the last twelve years, more than 12,000 leaders globally have applied it to expand their careers and lives in powerful ways as they embarked on their own journeys of personal evolution.

WAYFINDING THROUGH LIFE'S GROWTH MOUNTAINS

Throughout our journey in life, we experience a variety of Growth Mountains. Some are small; some are large. There are peaks and valleys across this mountain range, with some so steep and treacherous that we fear we may never make it to the top.

These mountains show up in our personal lives as different periods of growth and evolution, from our childhood all the way through our teen, young adult, mid-life, and even senior years in the form of key life experiences. Personal Growth Mountains encompass things such as navigating relationships, community involvement, parenthood, empty nesting, aging parents, our own physical and mental health crises, and more.

Other Growth Mountains are our professional ones that run the gamut from post-high school education to our early job experiences like my times at Johnson & Johnson and Bayer. They go from entrepreneurship or career advancement to climbing that proverbial career ladder or lattice, becoming a people manager, a managing director, a vice president, all the way up through retirement and reinvention.

And of course, our journey doesn't take place on one single mountain or even on one mountain range. Over the course of our lifetime, we hike from mountain to mountain, terrain to terrain, and sometimes even circle around to opposite sides of the same mountains to explore, learn, and grow.

THE GROWTH MOUNTAIN PRISM

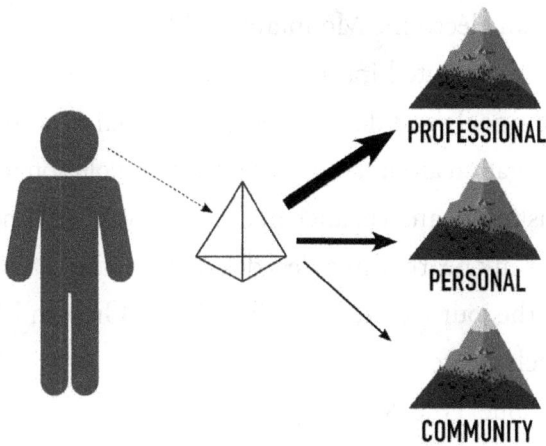

When you experience something new, different, or challenging in your personal life, you likely find yourself on a brand new Growth Mountain. As you explore your career and identify your purpose, you may discover you're on another mountain. You are likely to move back and forth between these mountains, traversing the one that is most important at any given time.

Our ancient ancestors used the art of Wayfinding as their method for traversing new territories and scaling the mountains along the way. **Wayfinding is building your map as you go.** In every country and every continent on earth from the beginning of time, we traveled together, heading out across new lands. We learned the weather patterns and the seasons, the predators and the dangerous terrains. Throughout our journey, we often found Mountain Guides along the way who could give us guidance for our trip—what berries to avoid, the safest spot to hunker down during a storm, and even what things are smart to pack for the new region we were headed toward next.

While our modern society is accustomed to having what amounts to an electronic Mountain Guide of sorts with our GPS apps and AI-generated insights that provide us with predefined routes to our goals and destinations, it's crucial to recognize that real-life navigation around our own personal evolution requires the more sophisticated and yet ancient approach you will find on these pages. Over my nearly three decades of coaching, I know this to be true: In the journey through life's diverse Growth Mountains, we must each create our own Wayfinding Compass, calibrated to our own unique True North.

After working with thousands of leaders at all levels around the globe, I can tell you this: Everyone's True North is unique to them and depends on where they are at an exact moment in their life. That is exactly why a book such as this can be incredibly helpful. It's not because I am endeavoring to provide you with a map of a well-designed life that will most likely become outdated tomorrow, but it's because the art of Wayfinding is a process, developing a compass of sorts. No matter where you find yourself, you can pull it out, orient back to who you are, and begin again. And the beautiful thing about a process is that once you know how to Wayfind, you can immediately embark on your own personal evolution journey—in leadership and in life.

The truth is that one-size-fits-all directions do not suit our different careers and diverse lives, especially when working and living in times of uncertainty like today. Instead, we need the tried-and-true art of Wayfinding, charting our course as we go. It is through this process that we acquire the essential "mountaineering" skills necessary to navigate the ever-changing complexities of our personal and professional experiences in a world that shifts by the moment.

Guided by our Wayfinding Compass, this Field Guide will explore the four cardinal directions of Self-Awareness, Self-Alignment, Self-Trust, and Self-Worth, and discuss how to find the guides we need along the way. Over my more than twenty-five years as a Coach, I have learned that no one successfully scales *any* mountain alone. In our personal growth journeys, we are ideally accompanied by not only our community of peers but also by three types of Mountain Guides—the Mentor, the Advocate, and the Coach.

THE GROWTH MOUNTAIN LANDSCAPE

Imagine for a moment the day you stepped off the stage from your high school or college graduation into the land of possibilities—a land full of new Growth Mountains you had never noticed before. As you look around, you realize you're in the lowlands, the plains surrounding the mountains. There are gorgeous wildflowers, cute animals, curiosities, and lots to explore out there in those Early Career Fields.

But there are also new dangers—sinkholes you wouldn't know were there until you walked into them or wild coyotes on the prowl for naive prey.

And often, as we move through our lives and careers, we yearn to see sights other than the open plains. Knowing the view is always broader—and usually better—from above, we choose a mountain that has piqued our interest. Maybe it's medical equipment sales, or maybe it's parenthood and marriage (three mountains I tried to scale simultaneously in my twenties)—and we start to climb. Now we find ourselves in more of a wooded, forested area slightly higher than the base.

In these woods, we find new things to explore that couldn't exist in the fields—gorgeous waterfalls and streams, new varieties of trees, and verdant landscapes. We discover beautiful foliage and wide-ranging temperatures on the north- and south-facing sides of the mountain. And of course, we find new dangers there too. We might come upon a cave with a family of bears inside. We might see plentiful and gorgeous red berries, and only after we eat them do we unfortunately discover they are poisonous.

Some people may happily choose to spend their entire lives in this forested area, what I refer to as Mid-Career Woods. Other folks try their hand at managing people and leave the life of an individual contributor behind, building campfires of connection and teaching new settlers how to live off the hilly land, which is decidedly different than the Early Career Fields.

And yet still others build and develop breadth and depth of expertise with the wildlife in the pine cove on the eastern side of the mountain. Or they become a subject matter expert in their passion area by focusing on a disease that's spreading among the willows in the west. In the case of our personal lives, we may venture to connect with a life partner, someone we can build a family with and a life together in the beauty of the woods.

After a time, many of us feel the tug to keep climbing to new heights, so we start moving up into the rocky, craggy area far above the treeline called the Summit. There, in comparison to the verdant forest, the vegetation is scarce. And on any given day there's as much chance we may meet a friendly old mountain goat as a clever mountain lion lying in wait for dinner. And because there are fewer people at this height on the Growth Mountain, it definitely starts to feel lonelier, a feeling compounded by the fact that we are more exposed than ever before. The wind whips us constantly. The sun burns us. But it is only at this level that we can see the unparalleled beauty of the breathtaking vistas below.

I often think of the Summit as the much more exposed area near the top of our Professional Growth Mountain, the domain of the managing directors, vice presidents, and officers of a company. Or in the case of our Personal Growth Mountain , this could be the stage of parenting when we become empty nesters, experiencing life with our partner while watching our kids "adult"—finding their own partners, careers, and lives—or even caring for our own aging parents. It is from this place that we can watch others scale the mountain terrain beneath us and share our own experiences or expertise. After all, we have been where they are and therefore have a unique and valuable perspective to share.

Let's go back to my story of tumbling down the mountain. Remember, I was just a few years out of college. Being launched into a sales manager role at Bayer was like a helicopter just dropped me off in the Mid-Career Woods without any acclimatization and, not surprisingly, without a Compass or Mountain Guides. I failed miserably.

My helicopter lift eliminated my opportunity for support and mentoring on my trek up to this next level. When I so spectacularly failed in my quest to become a people manager at the age of twenty-four, whose fault was it? While I am sure I was quite convincing in the interview process that I was ready to manage a team—I was a salesperson after all—I had zero relevant experience on my resume. Was it the company's fault? Should we have had a training program of some sort?

The truth is that it was more a perfect storm of circumstances. It was one that definitely impacted my journey to ultimately build two leadership development coaching and consulting companies with a focus on helping organizations develop their high-potential talent in inclusive and sustainable ways.

On the pages to come, I am excited to share how to navigate our Professional Growth Mountains using the ancient art of Wayfinding, which I will refer to as the Wayfinding Compass concept. Leading folks like you through their own personal evolution is what we have done with our PEER Technology Framework and Group Coaching experiences at EDGE Leadership since I founded the company in 2013. You can read more in my book *The PEER Revolution: Group Coaching That Ignites the Power of People*. But because I'm also in a phase of life where my Personal Growth Mountain is front and center, I will certainly sprinkle in some thoughts and suggestions for navigating those ranges too.

After all, we are *whole* people, my friends. Our Professional and Personal Growth Mountains overlap and together form a mountain range that spans our lifetime. It is time to turn leadership development inside out—the internal source from which our external behaviors are born. As I learned from my mentor Brené Brown as part of her inaugural global cohort of coaches bringing her Dare to Lead work to corporations in 2018, *who* we are is *how* we lead.

Are you ready to hit the road? Then grab your backpack, and let's go.

2

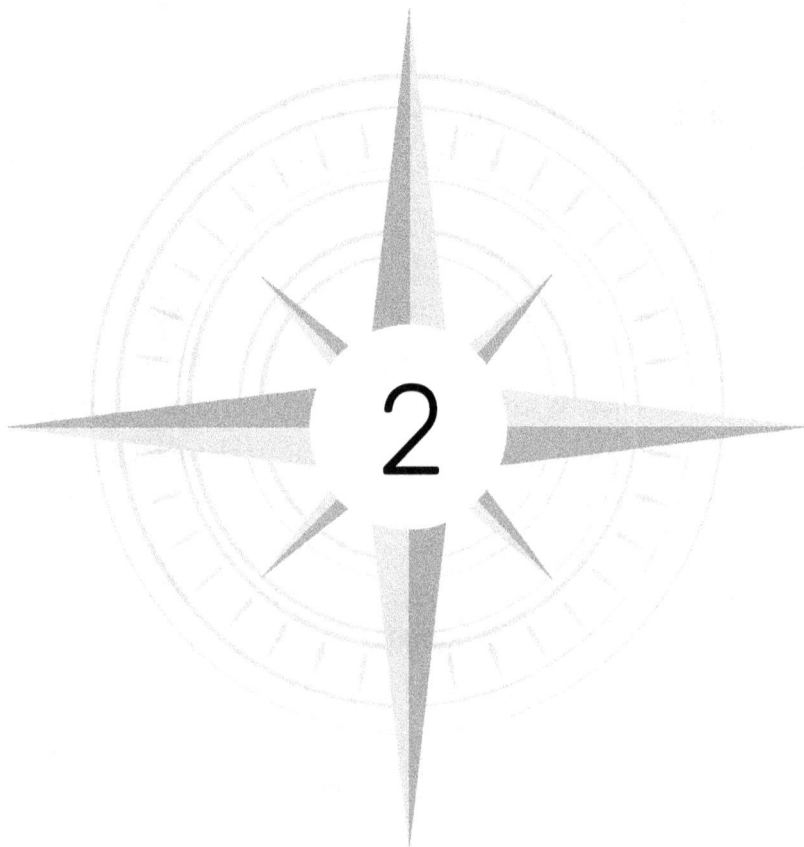

THE WAYFINDING COMPASS
Building Your Personal
Evolution Model

L ast summer, I hiked a glacier in Iceland with my husband,
Kevin, and our twenty-one-year-old son, Eli. It was our first
family vacation in three years. As someone who grew up in the city,
all I had to go on when we booked the experience was what I've
seen of glaciers in textbooks. And in aerial shots, glaciers look flat.

Guess what? They aren't.

In fact, Icelandic glaciers are on mountaintops and cascade down cliffs. (Did I mention I'm deathly afraid of heights?) I cried three times on our hike, once from sheer terror at the top and once from relief when I was back down and could hug Kevin. I have no pictures of the crying and no pictures of the fear, not because I am afraid to be vulnerable and share them but because I was too terrified walking on the ice to take my camera out of my pocket.

And if it seems like I'm inflating the experience, I assure you, I am not—even with a patient Glacier Guide who gratefully kept me talking about the most random things as we came down the mountain. Even after witnessing my tears at the top. Even beside the two men I love most in the world and who I know would do anything to keep me safe.

But here's the best part of the story. Snaking up in single file through the giant black sand dunes to reach the glacier face, I was sandwiched between Kevin and Eli, silently panicking at the slow reality that every step I took *up* would have its terrifying match coming back down.

And then I heard them.

Another team of six was making their way back down to the bottom from the glacier face and would have to pass us along the path that was not even wide enough for one person as far as I was concerned. I kept my gaze down on my boots, hands shaking, as I hugged the cliff. Then I heard a child, whose face I never saw since my eyes were fixated on my feet, shout out in a teasing voice—loud, bold, overconfident in youth—"Hey, Dad! Look at that scared old lady!" I immediately felt my cheeks and chest flush. Humiliation flooded me, and my mouth got dry.

But the wise dad didn't miss a beat. He replied in a beautifully even tone, "Oh, that's not a scared lady. That is a brave lady. Anytime you see someone who is afraid, remember that it's because they were brave first."

And that was the third time I burst into a puddle of tears on the Snæfellsjökull Glacier.

My friends, we can choose to walk through life mitigating fear. We can pile up pillows of protection around our bodies and hearts, around our children and our careers, around our marriages and partnerships. Or we can choose to feel the fear and live life anyway.

I promise that we can be both brave and afraid at exactly the same time.

Reclaiming our power is realizing that the only person dimming your light is you. As a mentor of mine once said, the only person coming to save you is the version of you that is sick and tired of the current version of you. Frustration ignites our desire to change.

External Mentors, Coaches, and Advocates are valuable (we'll talk later about how to enroll them as Mountain Guides in your Growth Mountain treks). But ultimately, we are our own best guides in this powerful journey called life. Only we understand the nuances of our challenges, experiences, and potential. Only we know how to maximize our momentum. No external resource can navigate our Personal and Professional Growth Mountains better than our inner Belly Wisdom. Your own True North will always be found within—in your gut, in your intuition, in your Belly Wisdom.

We must first be grounded in ourselves as deeply as possible to ensure that when we find ourselves off course as we navigate our Growth Mountains, we know how to efficiently and effectively calibrate back home to ourselves again. Thus, the Compass guiding us always points to ourselves first and foremost.

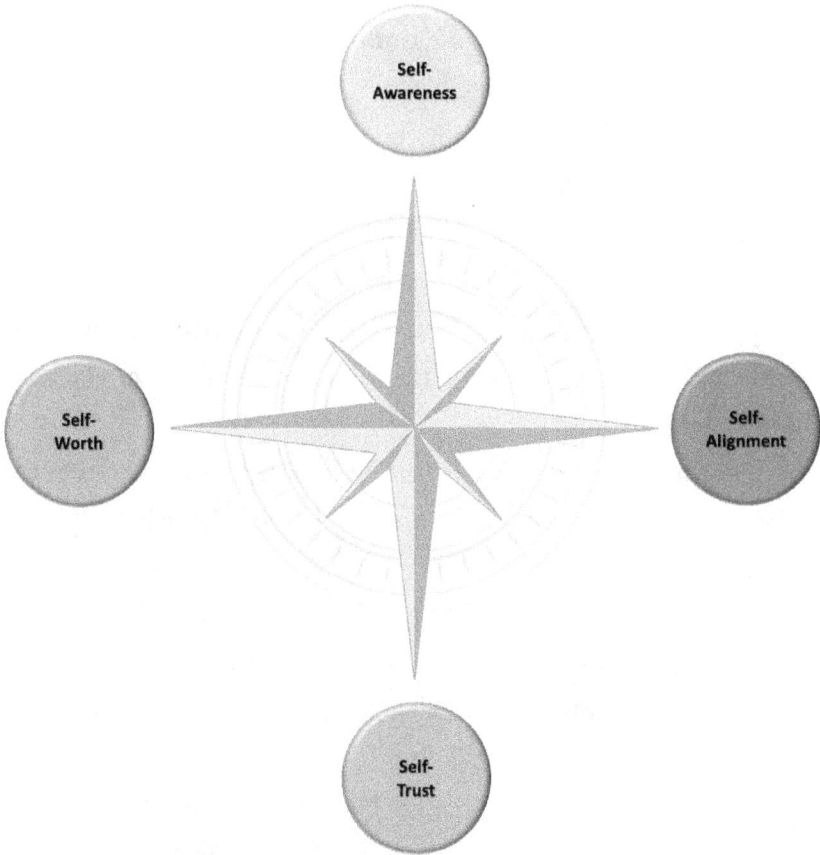

Like any compass, the Wayfinding Compass is made up of four cardinal points: North (Self-Awareness), East (Self-Alignment), South (Self-Trust), and West (Self-Worth). Each of these points represents an essential aspect necessary for personal evolution.

Starting with our North Compass point, we focus on **Self-Awareness**. This is measured by the genuineness of our opinions and the courage required to both express and sustain them. Self-Awareness is understanding who you truly are, what drives you, what you truly want, and where you excel. Moving clockwise, the East point of our Compass shifts to **Self-Alignment**. This is where we align our actions, values, and goals with intentional rest and recovery cycles so we can harness the energy needed to move forward with confidence and clarity.

Our South Compass point centers on **Self-Trust**. Self-Trust builds the courage in us to believe in our intuition and instincts, befriend our Inner Critic, and set and sustain boundaries to make bold decisions that matter. Here is where we practice self-compassion, take risks, and become loyal to ourselves. In other words, we learn how to treat ourselves as we would treat our very best friend.

Our final Compass point to the West forms the hub of our **Self-Worth**. This aspect focuses on recognizing and truly believing in the value we bring to the table and how that impacts our self-view, as well as how we show up to our families, friends, teams, and organization. Self-Worth is about intentionally reprogramming our internal (and often limiting) belief systems to one that serves us and our unique personal evolution journey.

While many books highlight Self-Awareness, few discuss Self-Alignment, and fewer still address Self-Trust and Self-Worth—and all are crucial for creating our own Wayfinding Compass. Every Compass must have the magnetic grounding of True North, which is why Self-Awareness is a vital yet often underrated leadership competency. Over two decades of coaching have shown me its importance. After all, everything else aligns from there. But Self-Awareness alone is insufficient. Early in my career as a Coach, I thought that the Wayfinding model of personal evolution was linear, that Self-Awareness leads to greater Self-Alignment. I thought the more I walked in Self-Alignment, the deeper I could build Self-Trust, and the stronger the foundation of Self Trust, the more powerful the sense of Self-Worth.

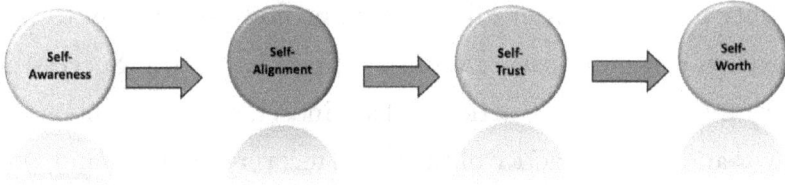

It has only been in recent years that I now see it as a circle—a spiral, to be exact—because as we deepen our learning, our evolution in each direction, we arrive at the next, but with new eyes to see. So the greater my belief in my Self-Worth, the more deeply I can dive into even greater Self-Awareness, the more I can walk in Self-Alignment, and on and on.

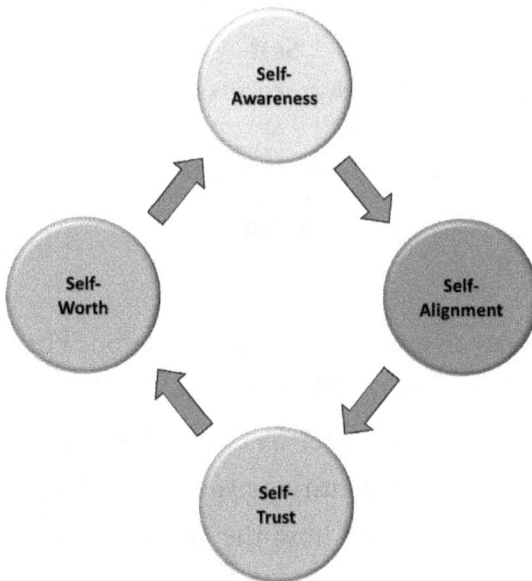

While most folks that we lead through our personal evolution group coaching experiences at EDGE Leadership begin at the northernmost point—Self-Awareness—the truth is that you can begin Wayfinding wherever you find yourself. That is the beauty of a circle after all. Each point flows seamlessly to the next—sometimes forward and sometimes backward. Successful Wayfinding is both an action and a mindset, a path we choose to travel and a daily practice of ritual and recovery. It's both/and, not either/or. It's evolution from the inside *and* the outside. It includes both the grueling, productive hike and the pause to refuel and refocus. Wayfinding is holding the tension of both.

NORTH: SELF-AWARENESS

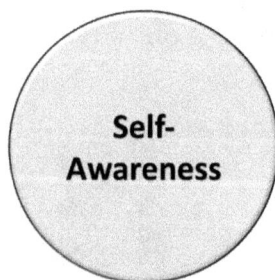

Self-
Awareness

WHAT

Self-Awareness answers the questions that our Hearts struggle with most: Who am I? What matters most to me? What do I want? What do I believe? What do I want to change? It involves the process of identifying your core values and personal purpose, acknowledging how the world and the people we choose to surround ourselves with have shaped (and continue to shape) us, and understanding how we do some of that shaping ourselves.

Self-Awareness requires contemplation, reflection, and soul-searching. The challenge is that our current world gives us very little space for introspection or stillness. But I promise you this: It is not a matter of just finding time for self-reflection. We must instead make it; we must create room with intention.

Self-discovery is often a good place to begin our journey into Self-Awareness. That is where we lean into vulnerability and curiosity, and focus on the *what*: what we are doing (or not doing) that is helping us along our Wayfinding path, and what is decidedly not. We ask, "What is working on this particular Growth Mountain? Why? What isn't? How so?"

Self-Awareness is also seeing clearly—perhaps for the first time—what we are thinking (our self-talk, if you will) and the impact it has on our choices. When we talk about the Head, the Heart, and the Belly, Self-Awareness is often aligned with our Head because it involves a lot of deep thinking and data collection.

Through Self-Awareness, we dive into our personal purpose—who we are at our very best—which enables us to articulate the impact we want to have on our world. It is our individual definition of what has meaning in our lives right now and always keeps the door of possibility open to evolve with us. Self-Awareness includes identifying our core values, our own personal leadership brand, and the means to articulate them—maybe for the first time in our life. It means understanding the belief systems that shape us and recognizing what we truly *want* versus the much more accessible what we *don't* want, or even the more familiar what we *should have* or *need* to do.

We will spend a good amount of time later in the book on the concept of belief systems, but I will say here that many of us have a self-limiting belief that "wanting" is bad or selfish. And I think it is important to challenge and ask, what if it isn't? For me, joy comes from not needing to perform, perfect, or people-please. In fact, through Wayfinding these last few years, I have discovered that most of my joy comes directly from following my "Wantings." Following what feels good, what makes me feel alive, awake, even sensual—food, conversations, movement of my body—creates an intentional attunement among my Head, Heart, and Belly.

My definition of attunement is simple: It's coming home to yourself. It is less of a learning and more of a remembering. It is remembering who you were before you became who you thought the world wanted you to be. For many folks, attunement is found in the journey of personal evolution.

The clues to your first signposts in calibrating your Wayfinding Compass to Self-Awareness are simple: follow your Wantings. They will lead you to your deepest desires, hopes, and dreams. They will uncover energy that you didn't even know you had, buried deep inside you, if you give yourself permission to lean into them.

Through Self-Awareness, we learn how to identify who we are, name our feelings, and understand our self-limiting beliefs and all the frustrating ways we self-sabotage. Then, grounded in this knowledge, we learn how to manage our energy and practice rest and recovery, which are key components of Self-Alignment.

For example, we can replace our self-limiting belief that "rest is laziness" or a "waste of time" or " has to be earned" with the knowledge that rest allows us to tolerate energetic discomfort—physically (think of an infant who doesn't sleep through the night for days on end), emotionally (a conflict with your in-laws), and mentally (a new boss or a possible layoff on the horizon). This builds resilience for difficult days on the journey (which always come), allows for growth and transformation, guides us toward unlocking our personal power, and sustains our momentum.

Self-Awareness is limited if it relies solely on "navel-gazing." When Self-Awareness is treated as a solo endeavor—with a book or a podcast instead of Wayfinding with peers—it fails. Rare is the individual who can understand themselves fully when not in relationship with others.

In fact, when we do not involve others in our introspection, we find that not only are we trapped by our own limiting belief systems but we often shortchange our possibilities with statements like these:

"I can't go for that promotion yet. I'm not ready."

"I can't go back to school. I don't have time."

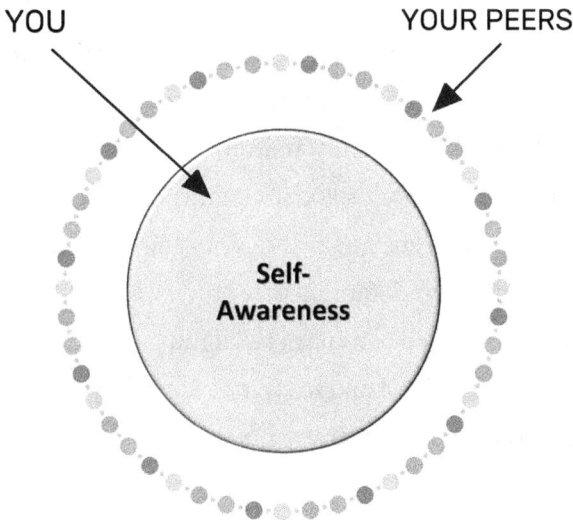

YOU   YOUR PEERS

Self-Awareness

When we introduce our peers as guides along our Wayfinding journey, we often find that not only do their insights and feedback challenge us to think bigger and bolder, but often they serve as powerful mirrors, reflecting the greatness we could not yet see in ourselves. Through the eyes of our peers, Wayfinding beside us in our Self-Awareness, we become an observer of ourselves.

EAST: SELF-ALIGNMENT

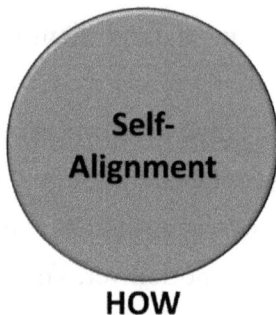

HOW

Self-Alignment is the ability to take the critical data from Self-Awareness and leverage it to begin aligning our choices more authentically with what truly matters to us. It assesses both our internal and external worlds and ascertains how well they are (or are not) serving our current goals and Wantings. When done well, it creates a level of internal stamina that provides the strength to handle the consequences of Self-Awareness. Aligning our actions, values, and goals with intentional rest and recovery cycles allows us to harness the energy needed to move forward with confidence and clarity.

If Self-Awareness is the *what*, then Self-Alignment is the *how*. It is the incredibly challenging and equally rewarding process of readjusting our daily choices to align them with our desired personal and professional growth. We align as we try on new behaviors for size. We fail, we try again, we build momentum, we practice—again and again. Self-Alignment is how we begin to move from the information collection of Self-Awareness to knowledge and prepare to move toward integration and embodiment. Self-Alignment incorporates daily behaviors, routines, and rituals that authentically honor our wants, desires, hopes, and dreams.

Self-Alignment is intentional practice, one that takes the information gained from Self-Awareness and applies it in practical and powerful ways to our daily lives. It is how we test-drive potential choices and behaviors, gaining greater clarity on our goals and priorities. It is where we inevitably struggle with shifting our actions—especially when we try to tackle this part of the journey alone—and often where we first become aware of our self-sabotaging efforts that keep us small and "safe." When we focus on how to bring about shifts in what we are doing or not doing, we find that we can begin to naturally and quite beautifully honor our desires and needs along our Wayfinding journey.

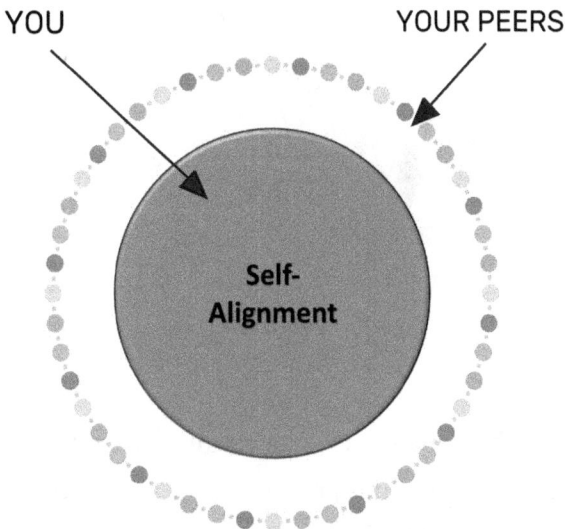

Just as our peers provide perspective and become a mirror through which we can better understand ourselves in Self-Awareness, they come alongside us in Self-Alignment as companions, coaches, and accountability partners. The folks we choose to journey beside often share best practices and lessons learned as we brainstorm possible next steps and solutions to our challenges. They also help hold us accountable to do what we say we want to do.

We begin going to the gym three times a week because we meet a friend there. We make healthier choices when snacking because our partner bought fresh fruit and cut it up into portions. In essence, our peers model the way, giving us permission to finally prioritize ourselves because *they* prioritize us.

SOUTH: SELF-TRUST

WHEN

Self-Trust is the consistency, challenge, and courage to pursue active experimentation. It is practicing and failing. And it is found in the resilience to get back up when we fall. Self-Trust is the *when* that follows the *what* and the *how* of Self-Assessment and Self-

Alignment. With this step, we move from our Head to our Heart because Self-Trust occurs when we not only know what matters to us but are also living in alignment with that knowledge.

Self-Trust is consistently treating yourself as well as you treat your very best friend. It is showing up for yourself when it matters to *you*. It is proving that you are dependable to yourself. It is the ability to honor your word—and keep it—to yourself. It is the ability to consistently meet your own needs. It is prioritizing your desires and your own needs and wants as much as you do everyone else's around you.

Self-Trust is the ability to be in direct conversation with your Belly Wisdom. It's knowing that when you are feeling some sort of way, you have the skill to stop, pause, and ask yourself, "What do I most want or need right now?"

And then give it to yourself.

Self-Trust happens when we focus on what really matters to us and practice self-compassion—empathy turned inward. It is quite simply the ability to feel self-disappointment without self-shame. In my world, we talk a lot about empathy as a leadership competency, and it's one of the primary ones we teach at EDGE Leadership. But in my experience, we can only offer empathy to others to the degree we offer it to ourselves.

Self-Trust is also about practicing equanimity—the art of feeling our feelings without getting carried away with them. It is intentional energy management—incorporating intentional periods of rest and recovery into your Wayfinding journey, just as you would include them in any mountain climb. It is no longer self-abandoning under the guise of taking care of others, as you will learn on the pages ahead. In my Wayfinding journey, this is the spot on my Compass that I struggle the most—boundaries with others and especially with myself.

In my experience as a Coach, it is also where most folks falter. We self-abandon all the time in our quest to be loved. Self-Trust done well involves cleaning up our self-talk and quieting our Inner Critic or what some refer to as imposter syndrome. It is recognizing the ways we self-sabotage and understanding where they came from. It is unflinchingly seeing how we often break our own damn hearts and leveraging that new knowledge to choose to show up differently.

It takes courage to fire up and become who you really are, to stop self-abandoning who you are (in the hopes of being loved by others) by becoming who you think they think you should be. Here is the spot on our Wayfinding Compass where we begin in earnest to rewrite our self-limiting belief systems and prepare for the reprogramming that happens in building Self-Worth. It is where we are able to see the stories we craft and live as truth across our Growth Mountains at work and at home. It's where we begin to rewrite the story, shift the limiting belief systems that no longer serve us, remove their power, and claim it as our own. We reprogram them, not unlike downloading the newest operating system to replace an outdated one on our phones.

Consistency is key to building Self-Trust, and as such, it is all about the *when*. It's showing up for ourselves weekly, daily, and sometimes even hourly. As we continue to practice, we learn the art of integration. That is where we can choose once again to rely on accountability partners in our peer group walking beside us, encouraging us to show up as our best self, providing empathy when we do not, and always guiding us back home to our favorite self.

WEST: SELF-WORTH

WHO

Self-Worth is about cultivating everyday hope and embodiment after integrating our *what* in Self-Awareness and the *how* of Self-Alignment, and practicing the consistency of the *when* in Self-Trust. This is the *who* of our Wayfinding Compass. Self-Worth isn't about *finding* ourselves. As one of my favorite mentors once told me, "Christy, personal evolution isn't about 'finding yourself.' You are not lost like a $10 bill left in last year's winter coat." Instead, this is the powerful space where we *meet* ourselves again.

In that way, Self-Worth is less of a learning and more of a remembering—remembering who you were before you became who you *thought* the world wanted you to be. Many of us grew up watching our parents cling desperately to the "right way" to live life—the right professions, neighborhood, even clothing choices. Our fears of losing connections with others are baked into our self-limiting belief systems as they were reinforced by coaches, teachers, and community leaders, and then later and even still today by our spouses, partners, and even our bosses and our children. We learned at our parents' knees to live our lives trying to satisfy what we perceive to be others' demands and learning to self-sabotage by suppressing the parts of ourselves that ultimately don't fit into that projection. And then we unwittingly do the same for our children. I know I certainly did. And so the ultimate Wayfinding journey is to find our way back home to ourselves.

Self-Worth is the space where we explore our feelings of not being enough. I have spent years of my life not feeling like a good enough daughter, wife, and friend. And don't even get me started on not feeling like a good enough mom or leader. Self-Worth is where I learn to accept "all my parts," where I am radically accepting my human imperfections and natural talents. As psychologist Richard Schwartz says, "When we learn to love all our parts, we can learn to love all people—and that will contribute to healing the world."[3] Through Self-Worth, we not only befriend the Inner Critic that bellows in our minds but also reparent our Inner Child.

Wayfinding the path to our worthiness is accepting and loving ourselves. Self-Worth is the radical acceptance of all of you—both the light *and* the shadow sides. This section of our Compass moves our personal evolution from our Head and Heart to our Belly. It is built on the consistent application of the skill of equanimity that we learn about in Self-Trust—the balance of feeling our feelings without being carried away with them. It is where we love and accept ourselves just as we are right now, even the shadow sides—in fact, especially the shadow sides.

Self-Worth is recognizing that our true power is found at the root of what we often consider our weaknesses. For me, it was the fear of vulnerability. I armored up—both at work and at home—to protect myself from feeling or, worse, looking vulnerable.

As I Wayfound my way through my own personal evolution, vulnerability became my greatest strength.

I would have never written this book even two years ago. Give a keynote and share my mental health struggle? Not a chance.

When I owned my vulnerability, my life was changed forever—both personally and professionally. As Brené Brown said on vulnerability, "When we deny our stories, they define us. When we own our stories, we get to write a brave new ending."[4]

Self-Worth is where we can now clearly see the self-limiting beliefs that are holding us back and reprogram our brain to see a different reality, one that has existed all along. It is where we move from Emotional Intelligence (EQ) to Energy Management. It is where we learn at the deep Belly level that we have the power to manage our mindset because there is a different voice than the brutal Inner Critic—a much quieter one that has also been speaking to us all along. It is where we honor our boundaries consistently and develop the ability to rely on self-compassion as our default from judgment. It is also knowing—trusting—that we can be okay when others are not okay with us, when life, our jobs, or our kids are not okay.

We gain knowledge by reading, watching, and hearing, which leads to Self-Awareness and Self-Alignment. We gain wisdom by *doing*, which leads to Self-Trust and Self-Worth. And while the Wayfinding Compass is based on our own wisdom, our wisdom is not enough on its own. Here's why. Adults evolve best when in community with others.

YOU   YOUR PEERS

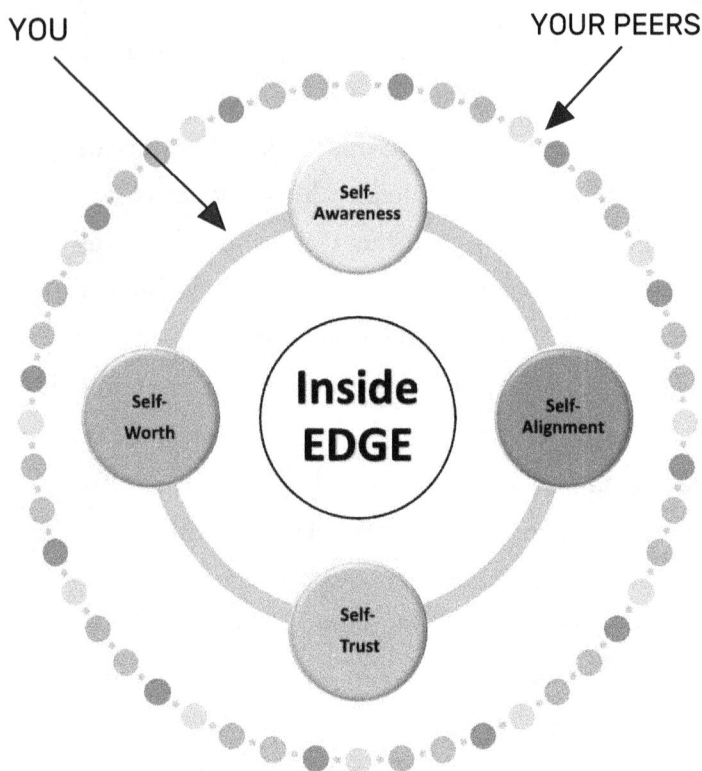

Think about it. Our Self-Awareness deepens with feedback and insights from those who know us best, and sometimes even with a random comment from a stranger. We were built to be mirrors for one another, shining back the greatness that is inside us that often we cannot see on our own. We can only feel belonging and connection—two basic human needs—in relation to each other.

In leadership, we often talk about the importance of self-respect because no one follows someone they don't respect. And no one respects someone who doesn't respect themselves. The truth is— and I have seen this over and over again in my coaching practice— if we don't like ourselves, we will be incapable of making healthy decisions. When we can generate *within* ourselves an emotional climate and steadiness, we can act consciously and with compassion for ourselves and for others. When we live and lead from a space of Self-Worth, when we can truly see and hear ourselves, only then can we create that same space for others. This space is what Harvard Professor Amy Edmonson calls "psychological safety," the belief that we are free to express our thoughts and concerns without fear of negative repercussions.[5]

We cannot manage well-being and Self-Worth through an app. We won't find it in a prescription. We can only curate it through authentic relationships with one another, through connection, co-regulation, and the creation of Third Spaces. Wayfinding is essentially a human task to find our way home to ourselves again. And as I have learned firsthand, it is much less of a learning and more of a remembering. True Self-Worth means accepting yourself for who you truly are—not for who you wish you were or who you still want to be. For me, it involved Wayfinding back to my inner child. When I began, I thought I needed to heal her, but what I learned was that she did not need healing. I did.

3

SELF-AWARENESS
Finding Your True North

"I don't even know who I am anymore or what matters to me." I recently became an empty nester, and let me tell you, that transition rocked my world. Kevin and I only have one kid, and if you had asked me when Eli was eight, twelve, or even sixteen how much of my life was focused on parenthood, I would have said only part of it. In fact, I would have proudly informed you that my life was so much more than "just being a mom." If I am honest, I had ill-informed biases against stay-at-home moms.

I recall saying things like this: "I'll be fine when he goes to college. I have so many other aspects to my life. I am a business owner and a Coach, and I have my work and my writing. I have my board work. I volunteer in the community. I have a great circle of friends."

All of that was true, but then Eli left for college, and I fell apart.

It was as if the puzzle piece of "mom" was not only way bigger than I expected but had somehow become the centerpiece of my puzzle that everything else—work, volunteering, and more—plugged into.

I know this is not unique to me. Consider how many people online have handles such as Eva'sMom, SpicyMama, or HandyDad.

Most of us would agree that parenthood is a very big Growth Mountain of its own. We start out in the Early Fields of managing infancy and toddlerhood, and then we move on to the Mid-Life Woods of raising preteens and (gasp!) teenagers. Fortunately, the Wayfinding skills build on one another for a lot of it. What worked during toddlerhood supports and buttresses our choices as we raise elementary school kids, and the best practices for raising a preteen build on that. I assumed that parenting a young adult would be the Summit of the Parenthood Growth Mountain for me.

But it wasn't.

I wasn't at the Summit. All the ways we parented a teen no longer worked when Eli moved five hours away and began to build his own life at college. And I started realizing that maybe I was at the base of a whole new Growth Mountain. I realized that my sense of Self-Worth was tied to being a parent in ways that had been entirely invisible to me. It was tied to being "needed."

Through Self-Awareness and by sitting *with* my depression (not *in* my depression—two entirely different things) and sharing what I found with my own peer group, a beautiful mirror of a friend reflected something that uncovered one of my self-limiting beliefs: "I am a good mom only when I am needed."

This tracks the journey of raising a child, right? We are taught that you have to put your children first and foremost. Their mental well-being is above our own. Their physical needs come first. And what I learned was that I was only okay when my son was okay. And when he wasn't? Honestly, I was pretty much an f'ing mess.

I realized that I had allowed our mother-child relationship to become one of enmeshment and that it was time to set some boundaries. And I don't mean boundaries with *Eli*. I mean boundaries within *myself*. I had to decide how often I would think of him—especially when he was in times of struggle—or worry about him.

Because what if on the Growth Mountain of parenting a young adult, my being a good mom wasn't being needed? What if I was a good mom when I *wasn't* needed?

Whew!

This is the power of upgrading our internal operating system. Our belief system can literally change in a moment. At any time, we can take the updated information in front of us and choose to believe something new.

And as I started my journey on this new Personal Growth Mountain of Parenting a Young Adult, I knew I needed to calibrate my Wayfinding Compass through Self-Awareness. And I wanted answers. What is my True North? Who am I? What do I believe? What do I want? After all, Self-Awareness begins with understanding who you truly are, what drives you, what you truly want, and where you excel.

WAYFINDING BASICS: WHO ARE YOU, AND WHAT DO YOU WANT?

The first signpost toward Self-Awareness is reflection. The invitation is to get curious about yourself but avoid judgment, and do it all by leaning into vulnerability. As Brené Brown emphasizes, vulnerability is the foundation of innovation. Prepare intentionally for your Wayfinding journey. Identify steps to take—those you can do alone and those needing support from Mentors, Coaches, or Advocates. Carve out time for introspection, even if all it can be is thirty minutes a month to start.

Remember, you're reflecting on who you are right now—not who you were five years ago or who you want to be five years from now.

✦ FIELD NOTES

I invite you to grab a journal or open the notes app on your phone and title it Wayfinding: Self-Awareness. Ask yourself: What are my core values? What is my personal purpose? What impact do I want to have on the world? Who am I at my very best?

One of the best curiosities is answering this: Who is my favorite self?

As I reflected and asked myself these questions, I discovered that my top core values are authenticity, connection, and innovation. My personal purpose is to connect people back home to themselves by building spaces for vulnerability and empathy, where they feel like they belong. My favorite self? Well, first, she doesn't wear any makeup (fascinating, right?). She is well-rested, very present, and peaceful.

Take your time as you explore and reflect. Like my no-makeup note above, allow yourself to be surprised with what comes out as you write without judgment. Remember, there is no "right" answer—just *your* answers. Don't rush through this step.

Okay, now that you have an idea of *who* you are, the next question to ask yourself is this: What do you *want*? At first, you may find you are clearer about what you *don't* want than what you *do* want. Please know that it's completely okay to start there and work back.

As I embarked on my Wayfinding journey of personal evolution, I realized that when Eli went to college, I wasn't sure who I was and what I wanted. I had allowed myself to be so consumed by work and parenting that I didn't have any hobbies, unless of course you count scrolling on my phone a hobby. If you looked at my phone stats, you'd see that I spent an average of five hours each day on my phone. So I declared 2024 my Year of Me. At forty-six years old, I was ready to focus on loving myself—for the first time since I was a little girl.

And interestingly enough, even before I declared this as my goal that February, I had already created my vision board on New Year's Day, which included cutting my board into the shape of a heart, putting my *own* picture on it, and for the first time in my ten years of doing this annual reflective activity not including on it any reference to my role as a parent. I knew that after eighteen months into my journey of being an empty nester, 2024 was also about allowing Eli the space to live his own life and repurposing the energy that he no longer needed from me back to myself.

IDENTIFYING SELF-LIMITING BELIEF SYSTEMS: WHAT DO YOU BELIEVE?

The next signpost on our Wayfinding journey toward Self-Awareness is figuring out what we believe and identifying the self-limiting belief systems that can hold us back and keep us stuck. By exploring your belief systems and the ways you self-sabotage, you can then rewrite the story. And just like carrying more baggage for the journey ahead than is needed, you won't get very far on your mountain trek carrying more than you need. Our mindset—what we believe to be true—is based on our belief system. And those belief systems create the stories we write about the world, others, and of course, ourselves.

I invite you to think about our belief systems as our operating software—usually installed long ago and often very outdated. Belief systems are totally invisible to us but binding in powerful ways. When we understand them, we not only clearly know what we want and don't want in our lives, but more importantly what we believe and how we get in our own damn way. And when we understand what we believe, we understand what needs to heal and grow as we evolve.

The research on nervous system regulation tells us that our bodies have the ability to process 11 million bits of information per second, yet our brains can only process 40 bits per second.[6] So our Head must filter life, experiences, people, and conversations through our belief systems. To filter out the other 10+ million bits of information per second, our subconscious brain asks itself, "What should I focus on here?" and "What *really* matters?"

As I mentioned in the Introduction, our brain is a pattern-seeking machine. In 2024, I bought a matte gray car. I was really on the fence because I had never seen a car that color before. But after I purchased it, I saw cars in that color everywhere. In this way, our brain is similar to a mirror. It reflects the beliefs we repeat, the thoughts we emphasize, the patterns we focus on.

Do you believe you aren't good enough? Your brain will find proof. If you keep telling it you "don't have enough time," that will become your reality. If you keep looking for what is "wrong" with your body in the mirror, it will highlight every flaw, not because it is true but because you are unconsciously filtering reality based on your internal belief system.

But if you train yourself to focus on what's working, what's growing, and what's possible, your brain will instead show you those things. Our beliefs tell our brains what to scan for and focus on, and our brains say, "Okay. Got it. Understood. Let me find more of that."

So if you keep telling yourself, "Nothing is working," "I don't have enough time," and "No one cares," you are not *describing* reality—you are *creating* it.

Let me give you an example. In high school, my sophomore English teacher told me I was a bad writer. And I am ashamed to say that I carried that belief with me well into adulthood. In 2021 when I started writing my first book, *The PEER Revolution*, I didn't believe I could do it because I saw myself as a bad writer. The story I told myself was that no one would read it and I would embarrass myself. (Side note: It became a bestseller.)

Similarly, I didn't work out regularly until after Eli went to college. Part of it was the self-limiting belief that I am not an athlete, that I am not fit, and that I am overweight. And the more I believed that, the truer it became. My words built my reality.

Language is generative. Our words, both what we say aloud to others and what we say inside our own heads—our self-talk—matter far more than we know. Believing something actually makes it true.

Below is a list of common self-limiting beliefs. I have personally believed most of them, and in some cases, I still do. Updating my belief systems is an ongoing journey that I will likely Wayfind across throughout my entire life. They are also ones I have seen in many clients over the decades in my coaching practice.

Read through and circle the ones that resonate with you. Then, as you reflect on what you believe, you can dive deeper into your journal for where they may have first entered your life, why they had value (at the time), and how you can let them go if (like me) you discover that carrying them no longer serves you—like an outdated OS for your phone.

My examples of self-limiting beliefs fall into five main categories.

1. Productivity = Self-Worth

▶ If I don't put the needs of others first, I will be alone.

▶ I am only worthy of _____ when I bring value. (My self-worth is tied to my productivity.)

▶ Fun is for children. I need to be serious to get ahead.

▶ Success is only earned through hard work.

▶ I am only worthy of success if I "earn it."

▶ Asking for help is a sign of weakness.

2. Being "Good Enough" = Fear of Inadequacy

▶ My mistakes/imperfections make me unworthy.

▶ Bad things don't happen to good people.

▶ I'm too _____ (old/young/quiet/loud etc.)

3. Worry = Control

▶ The more I worry, the more control I have.

4. Rest and Time

▶ I need to earn rest.

▶ Resting is unproductive or a waste of time.

▶ I don't have time for _____.

▶ Pleasure and/or prioritizing myself is indulgent or selfish.

▶ Taking up space is arrogant. Selfish.

5. Being Liked = Not Being Alone

► If I make myself small, people will like me.

► If I put others ahead of me, I won't be alone.

Are your own self-limiting beliefs reflected in some of my examples? What else comes up for you? Write it down.

My friends, whatever you believe becomes true for you. And just like our phone takes its cues from each new OS, we act according to our belief systems. If I believe that lawyers can't be trusted, I won't trust them. If I believe that men are cheaters, I'll move in and out of relationships often because of people who cheat. Change the belief system; change the reality.

As we evolve across our Wayfinding journey, we learn that personal evolution is less about our place in the world and more about our place in ourselves. It is not how everyone else views us but how we view ourselves. That's what really matters. The degree to which a person can grow is directly proportional to the amount of truth they can accept about themselves without running away, numbing out, or avoiding. Self-limiting belief systems cause us to self-abandon, over and over again. All they truly do is bring us suffering—suffering that *we alone* cause ourselves.

When we can see that reality is not defined by our self-limiting belief systems, we can let them go and see them for what they really are: beliefs we took on and accepted without question from parents and systems that never actually served us. And we can, maybe for the first time in our lives, find peace.

⊕ FIELD NOTES

In reflecting on the self-limiting belief you circled above, I invite you to pull out your journal and ask, "What beliefs and activities would I like to change about myself? Am I willing to make the commitment to change them? What can I choose to believe instead?" Only in this rewriting process can we realize that we are not a character in our story but the author.

On my worst days—at my most insecure moments—I want to be the storyteller who is not defined by the story. Self-Awareness is being able to observe the story as separate from ourselves because when we shift or even reprogram our OS, we can dream a new, more aligned story into being.

REWRITING THE STORY BY FOLLOWING YOUR WANTINGS

Thinking about outdated operating systems, I had a moment of clarity in July 2024, nearly eighteen months into my journey as an empty nester. For the first time in my adult life, I realized it was time to prioritize my relationship with me. As of this writing, three years into my Wayfinding, I am finally feeling like I have found my footing again.

My old behaviors of putting everyone else first—and not just Eli but my clients, my friends, and my family—had left me depleted and fully in what most of us would call burnout. My energy was practically nonexistent. But I didn't know any other way to be. As I looked around, many of the people in my circle were feeling the same thing.

Without even realizing it, we were reinforcing these unhealthy behaviors of numbing out every time we talked about what shows we were binging on Netflix. We were drinking too much or having too many cannabis edibles—I've certainly done both. We were avoiding not exploring why we were deeply unhappy but posting "perfect" pictures on social media or working hard to look like we had it all together when we left the house. And oh, the *giving*.

I was giving everything I had (and even what I didn't) to others in the hope that as long as I did, I would be liked. Being *the* person everyone came to just reinforced my self-limiting belief that I was only worthy of love when I was needed, when I bring value to people. I had to release the story I told myself to release the pattern. When we recognize a self-limiting belief, we release its hold on us, and in that moment, we have evolved past it. And our personal evolution continues.

Let's take one of my self-limiting beliefs that "rest has to be earned." I used to treat rest as if it was a dessert, something to reward myself with after doing all the hard stuff. But research on nervous system regulation is very clear: rest is foundational, not optional. It enhances creativity, sharpens decision-making, and stabilizes emotions—essential skills in life and leadership. Once I started practicing rest daily, accepting that I needed and deserved rest just because I am human, my life became amazingly different. Now rest is not just allowed but prioritized daily.

One great example of this was creating a pillar of rest in my day each morning. I call it my morning ritual. My routine involves feeding my dogs and giving them their morning pets, having a latte in the same chair by the same window, lighting a candle, meditating, journaling, ideally watching the sun rise, and staying off my phone.

On an ideal day, it is two hours. On a busy day, it is still a minimum of a full hour. I do not compromise on this, even if it means getting up hours earlier to make the time. If I skip it, I know I am simply not able to function at my best. Our bodies have many systems that work together and impact one another. The health of our vascular system impacts our muscular system, our skeletal system, and our nervous system. You may be surprised to know that we also have an energy system. Terms like regulating your nervous system or accessing your parasympathetic system fall here. So for me, beginning my day slowly instead of rushing around sets up my nervous system in a grounded way.

Another great example of making time for rest is understanding and following what I call our Wantings. As I write this today, it is 2025, and I am officially at the midpoint of the Year of Me Part Two: Following My Wantings. This year, for the first time in forty-eight years, I didn't have plans on Mother's Day. As a kid, my role was to show up for my mom on Mother's Day. When I got married and had a mother-in-law, I added showing up for her on my to-do list. And when I had my own kid nearly twenty-two years ago, well let's just say that it added a new layer of "shoulds" to my schedule. So now this day—in my mind at least—was not only about what a good daughter or a good daughter-in-law should do, but also what a good mom should do.

About five years ago, I began rewriting my story by adding in a joyous afternoon with my girlfriends on Mother's Day and slowly replacing the "shoulds" that I had given myself. As I went to bed the evening before Mother's Day this year, I realized that I had *zero* official plans, so I decided I would spend the day following my Wantings. Have you ever tried it? It's pretty simple actually. Here's what you do.

Ask yourself, "What do I want right now?"

Then *do that*.

I went to bed slightly giddy at the prospect of my Sunday unfolding exactly as it was meant to. When I woke up, I had a notification that I was off the waitlist for Pilates, so I started the morning there. I got to video chat with my kid—twice. And then I went to a Women Who Rock pop-up event downtown to support local, women-owned businesses where I treated myself to flowers, got my tarot cards read, and found an amazing retro cooler that is officially my new favorite summer accessory. As I was driving home, I stopped to surprise my ninety-two-year-old grandfather and was surprised to see my mom there as well. And all this was before three o'clock in the afternoon. It was truly one of my favorite days of 2025 so far.

The reality is that rewriting our stories along our Wayfinding journey takes work. Letting go of control, saying no, and slowing down demands trust—trust that the sky will not fall and the world will not end if you don't (fill in the blank with whatever self-limiting belief you have today at this moment). Trust that you *are* enough—just as you are right now. Trust that the Universe or God or whatever you choose to believe has your back and can carry the parts that you choose to set down. Letting go of what holds us back is not a weakness; it is an act of courage.

So how do we do this? It begins with Self-Alignment—practicing the skills that you now know you want to incorporate into your life.

4

SELF-ALIGNMENT
Building Your Vitality Voltage

I f someone asked you right now, "How are you today?" how would you answer? We all ask and are asked this question many times every day. Video meetings and phone calls alike begin with "How are you?" Conversations with friends and family start with the same question. Even encounters with the barista start off that way. So I'm curious. How do you answer?

If you are like me, you probably respond, "Great. How about you?" or "Fine, thanks."

But in truth, I'm not always "great" or "fine."

So why do we always respond that way?

As I have gained confidence in my own personal evolution journey, I have found that I now respond to the question "How are you?" very differently. Instead of being on autopilot when I answer, I now pause before I speak and ask myself, "How am I right now, really?" Applying the practice of Self-Awareness, I give myself the gift of a moment of reflection before responding.

It can be awkward at first to pause when we're conditioned to answer without thinking. Most of the time, I explain to the other person so they understand what I am doing. For example, if you asked me that right now, "How are you, Christy?" I would most likely respond, "Hmm. Good question. Give me a minute to check with myself and see."

Once I've paused and asked myself the question, I stay open and see what bubbles up. Then I give myself permission to lean into vulnerability and share whatever part feels appropriate, given who I'm talking to at the time.

If Kevin asked, I might say, "I'm feeling conflicted by the pressure of finishing the new Inside EDGE group coaching program and meeting the damn book deadline and not leaving anything important out of either. I am feeling pretty much totally inadequate and completely overwhelmed."

To my local barista or Pilates instructor, I might just say, "I'm not at my best today, to be honest. How about you?"

Either way, when I answer authentically, I find that two very important things happen consistently. First, I realize I don't always know how I actually am. Remember that Self-Awareness is a life skill that needs to be cultivated like any other. So by pausing and asking myself, sometimes I am surprised at how good I am feeling, something perhaps I didn't even notice in my busyness that day.

Or conversely, if I am overwhelmed and say so aloud, then I am faced with the need to practice authentic Self-Alignment. If I'm truly not okay, I have to ask myself, "What are you going to do about that, Christy?"

When I'm feeling overwhelmed, what helps me most is moving my body and eating something—usually raw vegetables—both of which fuel my body, clear brain fog, and help me lock in and focus. But before I learned to practice the Wayfinding skills of Self-Awareness and Self-Alignment, I was so disconnected from my body that I didn't even understand how much the types of foods I eat impact my ability to think critically, problem solve, or innovate. In fact, one of the unintended consequences of my own personal evolution journey through Self-Awareness and Self-Alignment has been the shift in my relationship with food.

The second important thing that happens when I pause and answer authentically is that I create a more genuine connection with the other person. In fact, I have lost track of how many times I have said "I'm just okay today" or "I'm not at my best." Then a tangible relief washes over the other person's face, and they sigh quietly and say, "Me too." After that, the conversation takes off in a more connected way than would ever have been possible if I had just responded with "Great." And since connection and authenticity are two of my top core values, I get to fully walk in alignment with what matters most to me—powerful practices indeed.

REPLACING SELF-LIMITING BELIEFS AND BAD HABITS WITH INTENTIONAL CHOICES THAT SERVE US

Self-Alignment sits on the East point of our Wayfinding Compass. As the sun rises in the east, it reminds me that every day is a new day to begin again, to walk in alignment and authenticity. So what if yesterday wasn't great? What if I didn't show up well in the ways that matter to me? Did I snap at Kevin? Did I fall into old self-sabotaging behaviors? I can begin again each day with a fresh slate if I choose.

Self-Alignment is the process of readjusting our daily choices so they align with our desired personal and professional Growth Mountains. It mirrors nature—never static, always evolving. Wayfinding is not a masterclass in personal development. It's about evolving. As humans, we are made to evolve. And evolution by definition is continuous. It's a journey, not a GPS destination powered by generative AI. Life doesn't work that way. Wayfinding is building your map as you go.

The traditional definition of attunement is to be receptive or aware, or to make harmonious. Building on what I outlined in Self-Awareness, my definition of attunement is to tune into who we *are* by remembering who we *were* before we became who we thought the world wanted us to be. Attuning to our energy—our life force, our Vitality Voltage, if you will—can only come about through the process of discovery, experience, exposure, and connection to others, and just as importantly, to ourselves.

Attunement begs for movement. For interruption. For evolution. When we intentionally choose to create the actions to attune back home to ourselves—to what we truly want and value versus what we think we "should do" or "need to do" or "have to do"—we have a much better shot of navigating the gap between where we are and where we want to be in our lives, personally and professionally.

There are no shortcuts to this. Attuning by definition invites us to Wayfind and take the slower, more scenic path. We have to be ready to make shifts as needed along the way just as the people and the world around us shift. The terrain on our Growth Mountain is filled with challenges, obstacles, and hazards. It changes moment by moment as we go. Our Wayfinding is less either/or and more both/and. It is holding the tension between making purposeful choices to rest so I have the energy and clear head to forge ahead and take intentional action when it is time. The Wayfinding journey, when done well, incorporates work *and* ease, energy *and* stillness, internal *and* external—Head, Heart, *and* Belly. It supports the evolution of the Self that we were meant to become. That we have always been. That we simply forgot.

As we move toward Self-Alignment in our Wayfinding journey, our aligned path forward includes two Wayfinding signposts. First is fostering intentional action by plugging into our energy source and building our Vitality Voltage. The second is remembering that Rest = Energy.

PLUG INTO YOUR ENERGY CHARGERS TO BUILD YOUR VITALITY VOLTAGE

Understanding and cultivating our energy is crucial as we Wayfind on our Growth Mountains. After all, it's hard to hike very long on an empty stomach. Like all compasses, our Wayfinding Compass is magnetic, but instead of North and South, the poles are healthy masculine and feminine energies that everyone has regardless of where we are on the gender spectrum.

Having access to them and realizing what is unhealthy within them is key to calibrating our Wayfinding Compass by aligning them. When we see the metamorphosis of a caterpillar to a butterfly, we often think of the process as a simple transition, but it is decidedly not. The caterpillar must first dissolve itself into liquid goo before it can be transformed into something brand new.

The masculine is the Action. The feminine is the Pause. We need both poles when Wayfinding. Together they create alchemy where the resulting sum is greater than its parts. Throughout 2023 when people asked me how I was, I found myself responding using this analogy of the butterfly's metamorphosis. I can recall saying, "I have been the goo the last year, but now, something is different." It felt almost like I was fully formed but still inside the cocoon, just waiting for my time to break out.

Personal evolution is a type of transmutation. Through it we become something new and greater than we were. Both Self-Awareness and Self-Alignment are associated with healthy masculine energy. Healthy masculine energy is the energy of *do*-ing. I call this "muscling energy." It is bold execution. Courageous. Intelligent. Disciplined. Stable. It has an element of protection and powerful forward momentum.

In contrast, Self-Trust and Self-Worth pull from a different energy source—the healthy feminine. This is the energy of *be*-ing. It is reflective. Soft. Seductive. Creative. It is the space of rest and recovery. It is every bit as powerful as the masculine but in a very complementary way. It is intuitive, knowing and being able to easily access our Belly Wisdom. And it includes equanimity—the art of feeling our feelings without getting carried away by them.

After Wayfinding through Self-Awareness and now that we are clear on our core values and who we are and what we want, it is time to begin replacing the behaviors that no longer serve us with ones that do. As I was struggling with depression from 2018 to 2023, I discovered that it was actually a powerful time to explore my belief systems. We often look at depression and anxiety (and I have suffered mightily from both in my life) as though they are "problems to be fixed."

In reality, they can often be more like a fire alarm letting us know that something important in our life is off course and decidedly out of alignment. These signals point to the fact that we are not walking in authenticity and that we have healing to do. John Delony introduced this analogy to me in his book *Redefining Anxiety*. He said that if a smoke detector was going off in your house, you wouldn't cover it up with a pillow and keep going on with your life. You would use it to find the damn fire and— Put. It. Out.[7]

This winter, I had the opportunity to practice my Self-Awareness and Self-Alignment skills in front of a live audience. I had just launched the pilot of our new group coaching experience on personal evolution called the Inside EDGE with 100 leaders across the country. At the very first virtual session with one of the cohorts, I ended up looking completely incompetent. If you know me, you know that is my greatest professional fear. About four minutes after we were scheduled to begin, I realized something was very wrong. The video conference platform had placed me and one other person in a separate virtual room with everyone else in another one.

To say I got derailed in the moment is an understatement. I realized I could actually feel my heart beating and my breath turning shallow—telltale signs that my nervous system was becoming dysregulated. But here's where my Wayfinding skills kicked in. Because I was aware of the intrusive thoughts in my mind and feelings of inadequacy flooding my body, I wasn't entirely swept away by them like I have been so many times in the past.

And by the end of the two-hour group coaching session, I was able to joke with the cohort that maybe the Universe wanted to provide them with a front row seat to one of the skills I hoped to share with them over the next seven months. When life happens (and it will), we have far more choices to respond than we know. We have the opportunity to ground ourselves by practicing resilience and self-compassion, and in doing so we can walk in authentic alignment.

After the session, I did two important things to act with intention. I plugged back into my energy sources and increased what we call here at EDGE our Vitality Voltage. First, I called Kevin. The best antidote to shame (feeling like I'm not good enough) is empathy. Next, I hopped in the car and went to a Pilates class to move the unwanted energy generated from the experience out of my body.

After doing both, I was still embarrassed, but I was also fully grounded and plugged into two crucial energy sources for me: connection and movement. I was proud for not falling back into my old, self-sabotaging habits of belittling myself and ruminating. After all, getting dysregulated in the world today—at work and at home—is simply part of the human experience. What matters most is what we do next.

To be clear, I am not suggesting that we forgo modern medical conventions such as therapy, psychiatry, and prescriptions to support our mental health. I certainly have benefited from all of them. But what if there is more we can do? What if instead of looking at our emotions as problems to be solved we come alongside them and listen? As Delony says, what if we focus on the fire and not the smoke?

I ultimately found that managing my life force—my Vitality Voltage—wasn't found in Self-Awareness but in the Self-Alignment that came next. Now that I have a base-level understanding of my self-sabotaging behaviors and my self-limiting belief system, the Wayfinding best practice is to replace the bad habits and patterns with new choices that serve. It is understanding what both drains or depletes our battery, what charges it up, and how we can actively assess and answer the question "How are you, *really*?" with facts to back it up.

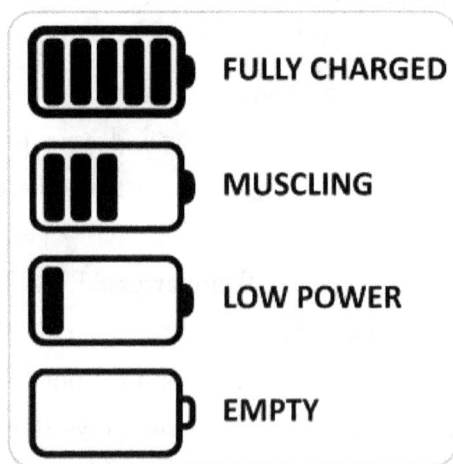

FULLY CHARGED

MUSCLING

LOW POWER

EMPTY

Are you operating at 100 percent and fully charged today? If so, this is the day to tackle that big vision project.

Are you at the Muscling through level? Maybe you'll choose to get out of the office and go for a walk at lunchtime.

Are you at the Low Power mode? Well, that's when I start rescheduling meetings because even if I am there, I'm not "there." And what would take me three hours to do on Low Power mode I can probably do in forty-five minutes when I am fully charged.

The trouble is that most of us lack the Self-Awareness to even know what our Vitality Voltage level is. And without Self-Awareness, we can't make the choices necessary for Self-Alignment.

⊕ FIELD NOTES

I invite you to ask yourself: What brings you energy? What depletes it?

Humans are incredibly complex creatures, and yet we are also very simplistic. We run on energy—our life force. In Reiki, we call it chi or qi; in yoga, it is called prana. In fact, there is a word for it in literally every culture on earth. When we live an aligned life—a fulfilled life—we have full access to our human vitality. And when our energetic battery hits Low Power mode, just like with our phones, our level of experiencing life is temporarily reduced as our bodies and souls work overtime to conserve energy and extend our battery life.

Once we assess our energy levels in the different aspects of our life, we can then begin to assess *who* and *what* depletes it and make intentional choices from there. The *who*, by the way, can be both external (a boss, a neighbor, a relative) and internal (an Inner Critic or an internalized voice). The *what* can be things we do (manage microaggressions in a meeting) or things we don't do (skip the gym to work overtime). And some choices **deplete** our batteries in healthy, productive ways. For me, it's writing, gardening, or exercise. After all, our batteries are meant to be used and recharged. But other choices can **drain** our batteries—sometimes entirely—just like leaving your phone out on a hot summer day. For me, the big one is scrolling through social media. I can lose ninety minutes in a heartbeat and still feel entirely exhausted at the end of it.

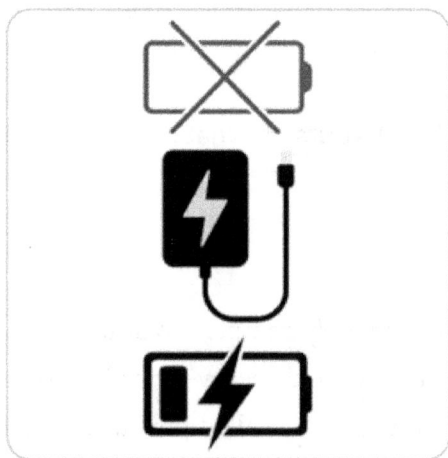

Our bodies are brilliantly designed to withdraw from anything that has become unsafe for us. A self-protected nervous system is an intelligent nervous system that is doing exactly what it was designed to do—keep us safe. And when we're drained from overextending ourselves, it can be incredibly challenging to connect with the world around us, especially when our bodies believe it is dangerous to do so.

As I said before, our Vitality Voltage can be depleted in good ways and drained in less helpful ways. Either way, we need to know what our energy sources are and plug into them with intention and Self-Awareness. And we need to identify our peers who will help us in our Self-Alignment. We do not change behaviors on our own. We change them in relation to others. The human body is built for connection, togetherness, and co-regulation.

Most of us simply do not have the discipline to change on our own. So what's the hack I learned on my own personal evolution journey? Find a peer to walk beside you. Once you have identified what you want to change, then you really only need two things. You need a thinking partner to help you move through the details of what to change and explore possibilities of how you can sustain it, and you need an accountability partner to walk beside you and ensure that you continue to prioritize those changes in the midst of everything else in your daily life. Sometimes these two peer guides can be the same person, and sometimes not. Either way, these guides are critical.

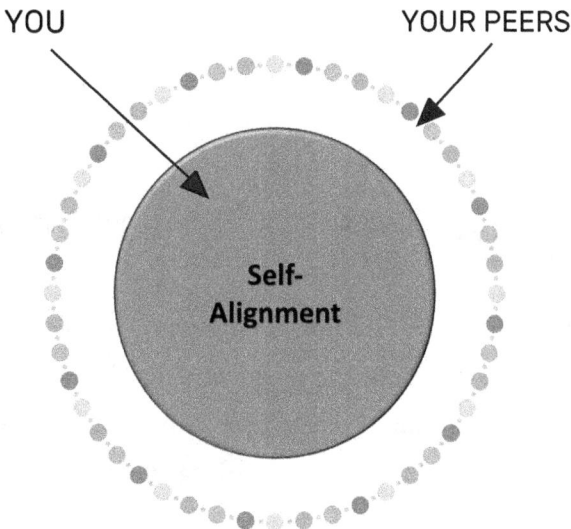

YOU   YOUR PEERS

Self-Alignment

Continuing on with the fact that language is generative, once we say (aloud) to someone who has earned the right to hear it that we are sick of our own BS, that we are unhappy, that we want to show up differently in our lives at work and at home, things can't help but change. Now we have accountability partners beside us as we strive to walk in more alignment.

The real work isn't working hard but knowing what to work on. Our peers provide perspective and become a mirror through which we can better understand ourselves in Self-Awareness. And then in Self-Alignment, they give us permission to prioritize ourselves because they prioritize us. A circle of trusted peers is absolutely critical in our Wayfinding journey because breaking down self-limiting beliefs is far easier with the power of peers.

My Wayfinding peers helped me increase my Self-Awareness that I was living my life according to the self-limiting belief that I am only okay if others are okay around me. I had no foundation of energy for myself at all, and a peer of mine asked me, "What would it look like if you put yourself *first* for an entire year?"

And as I mentioned, I did exactly that in 2024. And one of the biggest learnings I took from that journey had to do with redefining rest.

VITALITY VOLTAGE INDEX: REST = ENERGY

In their book *Burnout*, the Nagoski sisters describe the Human Giver Syndrome that defines people who feel "a moral obligation to give their whole humanity, and give it cheerfully."[8] If you're like me, this notion leads to the self-limiting belief that we are only worthy when we are doing for others, when we bring value. And that is a recipe for burnout. The best solution I found is focusing on regulating my nervous system by getting back into my body and recalibrating my Vitality Voltage.

When I first started studying energy in 2022, I realized that I hadn't taken care of my body physically in decades. I was out of shape, eating crap, never moving my body, sleeping poorly, and solidly in perimenopause. Most importantly, I felt like my battery was depleted entirely. I was, in essence, living every day as if I was in Low Power mode. That insight drove a deep Wayfinding exploration into nervous system regulation, mental health and well-being, and energy management. Eventually, it led to a multi-year Reiki certification to become a Reiki Master and the opportunity to support thousands of people on their own personal evolution journey. Of course, our EDGE grads all taught me way more on Self-Alignment than any course, book, or podcast.

Most of us have never learned the skills to manage our feelings. We hide from them, we run from them, and we numb ourselves from them. I have chosen all these bad habits myself instead of coping with my feelings at work and my feelings at home. But what if the issue in Self-Alignment isn't primarily about managing our feelings? What if our emotions are nothing more than the stories we write about the energy we feel?

If Self-Awareness is identifying our Wantings, then Self-Alignment is aligning our lives with what serves us and increases our inherent energetic Vitality. To manage our feelings and recharge our batteries, we must redefine rest. Contrary to all my self-limiting beliefs about rest, rest is not laziness, a waste of time, or something to be earned. As we discussed earlier, these are outdated belief systems that so many of us have been raised to believe, modeled by our parents whose parents modeled it for them. Too often, we are unwittingly modeling them for our own children.

Rest is not our reward for working hard. Rest is *Energy*. Rest recharges us and allows us to tolerate discomfort in our lives, something the world today requires a great deal of. There are different types of discomfort that in turn align to different types of rest.

- ► **Physical discomfort** can come from illness, chronic pain, lack of sleep, and injuries.

- ► **Mental discomfort** often comes from facing new challenges such as launching a new project, securing a promotion, taking a new class, or learning and practicing new skills.

- ► **Emotional discomfort** is felt when we grieve losses and change, when we have intrusive thoughts that are sad or anxious, when we worry about the past or the future.

- ► **Spiritual discomfort** is not necessarily connected to religious beliefs. It comes from living a life not authentically aligned with who you are and is often a lack of meaning and purpose.

Our ability to tolerate discomfort is the single most powerful self-regulation tool we can bring on our Wayfinding journey because it builds resilience and Self-Trust. It allows for growth and transformation, and it guides us toward unlocking our personal power. It is what helps us navigate life and leadership.

When we experience these discomforts and our energy levels are depleted—just like we would recover at Base Camps as we climb higher and higher on our Mountains—we need to respond by intentionally incorporating periods of rest in order to maximize our impact at work and at home in the following ways (most notably identified by authors Jim Loehr and Tony Schwartz)[9]:

> **Physical rest:** Getting enough sleep, eating nourishing food daily, moving our bodies.

> **Mental rest:** Any mindfulness act that is "nonthinking," which might include baking, gardening, painting, or other "single-tasking" activities.

> **Emotional rest:** Incorporates healthy vulnerable expression, including crying, journaling, talking with someone who can show up with empathy.

> **Spiritual rest:** This spans the gamut between intentional time in solitude (connecting to self and/or spirit) to acts of connection and belonging to others, including everything from intimacy to activism.

As you can see, rest is not just napping on the sofa, although that can be a great form of physical recovery. Periods of rest and recovery are a human energy source where we literally plug back into our energy. Given that these forms are common to all humans, knowing what type of rest we need at any given time is part of Self-Awareness. Acting on it, which includes giving ourselves permission to practice rest, is Self-Alignment.

⊕ FIELD NOTES

I invite you to grab your journal and answer the following questions:

What type(s) of discomfort (Physical/Mental/Emotional/ Spirtual) are you facing right now? How so?

What type of rest feels energizing to you right now?

Once we have the foundation of Self-Awareness to support creating a new belief system to counter our self-limiting ones, we can begin to align our choices to live more authentically at work and at home. And as we do, we will begin to realize that we have far more choices than we knew. For example, until I started becoming more aware of the fact that being on my phone drained my energy, I had no idea I was addicted to my phone. I never really saw my phone as outside of myself. I didn't go anywhere without it, certainly not outside the house, but even moving from room to room. Even as I write this now, my phone is beside me.

From a Self-Awareness standpoint, my peers' coaching and mentoring questions challenged me to see that mindfulness and mental rest were missing from my life, as well as plugging into daily physical movement. They challenged me to stop chasing "cheap" dopamine (the hits I get from scrolling on social media) and replace it with real dopamine—more play, community, nature, sunshine, meaning, and rest.

By incorporating their insights and feedback, I realized that the more I began to walk in Self-Alignment, the more I began to build Self-Trust. Instead of just saying I was going to work out, stay off my phone every morning during my morning ritual, and eat more raw vegetables, I actually started to do it. Self-Trust is showing up *for yourself* as much as you show up for everyone else in your life. And I can tell you that this point on the Wayfinding Compass was one of the most challenging for me on my personal evolution journey. Without my peers as my companions, I don't think I could have made it through.

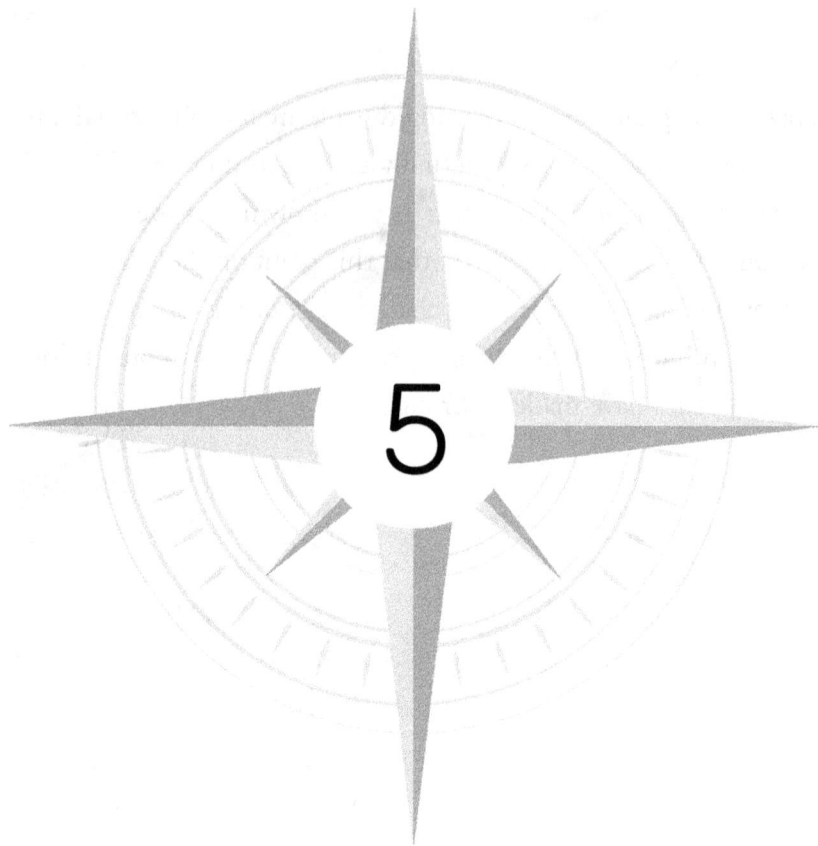

5

SELF-TRUST
Befriending Your Inner Critic

This past spring, great storms blew across the continental United States, and Pittsburgh got slammed with several microbursts. My township got hit incredibly hard, so much so that a state of emergency was declared, and we were without power for several days. At first, Kevin and I thought it was convenient to keep everything on the kitchen counter for easy access—the necessary scissors, battery packs, candles, and toothbrush, and the not-so-necessary broken flashlights, receipts, and sweatshirts. And like a computer with too many tabs open, the clutter started to drag me down.

In my regular, everyday life, I (mostly) put things away. I throw out my trash. I do my chores. But that week, I just didn't seem to have the energy. Living with my food in coolers and no Internet, hot water, or electricity drained my Vitality Voltage fast. And quickly, my inner life began to feel like my kitchen counter. Heavy. Cluttered. Overwhelmed. I recall standing in my disaster of a kitchen after thirty-six hours of no power thinking to myself, "I just have too many tabs open in my life right now."

My first reaction was to let my Inner Critic run wild. In fact, I could actually hear her nasty comments—critiques I would never dream of saying to anyone else but seem to flow so damn easily when directed to myself. There were judgments about my trashy kitchen, for stress eating an entire pack of chocolate Twizzlers, for buying said Twizzlers in the first place, and most definitely for bringing those Twizzlers to bed with me. And my Inner Critic was just warming up.

But instead of listening to that critical voice and falling down a shame spiral, I chose to extend the same level of compassion to myself that my awesome community offered me that week. I had friends who found me battery packs so I could get through eight hours of one-on-one coaching calls on my phone. Others offered a place to stay over the weekend. Friends brought me bags of ice, and friends brought me flowers.

Because I'm me, I started thinking about how working and living for three days in a home without power is a lot like managing our mental health. When life is smooth, my mental well-being is an afterthought. But when the storms arrive that drain all the power out of our batteries—like grief or chronic pain, a layoff, or a divorce—things can get out of control pretty quickly.

But through my friends' kindness, I was reminded of the power of allowing ourselves to receive care, love, compassion, and grace. Receiving is what we do when we give ourselves permission to "plug into" our energy sources. Receiving is a muscle, and especially for those of us who are far more used to giving, receiving gets easier the more we practice it, not just from others but from ourselves. Empathy turned inward is called self-compassion. And self-compassion builds Self-Trust, which could be the single most needed leadership and life-development skill to navigate this world right now.

Self-Trust is the consistent application of what we've learned through Self-Awareness and Self-Alignment. As we move from curiosity to action, we connect data to knowledge. Think of knowledge-building as connecting the dots, each dot a mile marker on our Wayfinding journey. Moving from one dot to the next forms our pathway to change and transformation across our Growth Mountains.

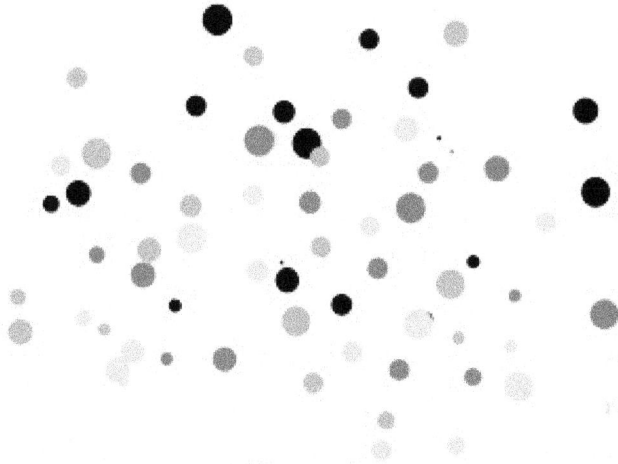

Information
(Self-Awareness & Self-Alignment)

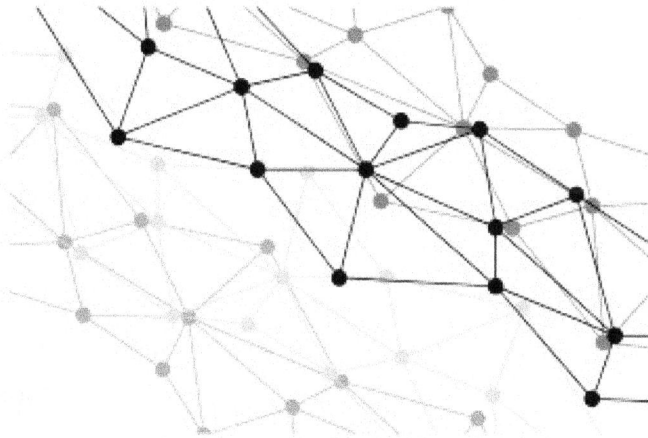

Knowledge
(Self-Trust & Self-Worth)

Integration is taking that knowledge and beginning to turn it into embodiment—wisdom. Self-Trust is the path paved with the bricks of changed behaviors and intentional choices around incorporating rest and recovery cycles into our lives. The shifts I made in Self-Alignment ultimately led me to the Wayfinding task of Self-Forgiveness.

After all, when someone in my life breaks trust with me, the best apologies include a change in behavior—intentionally choosing different actions. Self-Trust is no different. Because your relationship with yourself is the longest-lasting relationship you will have in your life, it benefits you to invest in it.

When I made my intention for the two Years of Me, I decided to make myself my own priority and honor myself as much as I did those I loved. I would treat myself and talk to myself as gently as I would my best friend. Self-Trust is not selfishness, no matter what my self-limiting beliefs tell me. Nor is it selflessness. It is, like most aspects of Wayfinding, finding the healthy tension between both. The goal is not to treat ourselves *better* than everyone else but with the *same level* of care we give others.

Self-Trust is the *when* of our Wayfinding journey, and that means consistency is key when we dive into this aspect of our Compass. Consistently prioritize your desires, your own needs, and your wants to the same degree you do everyone else's around you. It is treating yourself—and your priorities—as you would those of your very best friend. It is proving that you are dependable to yourself. It keeps you focused on what really matters and involves practicing the Wayfinding competency of self-compassion. Empathy is a much revered leadership skill and one of the primary ones we teach at EDGE Leadership, but we can only offer empathy to others if we offer it to ourselves.

When we have a strong level of Self-Trust, it is because we have a consistent (but not perfect because we are human after all) practice of regulating both our energy and our emotions. Self-Trust comes from knowing who we are (Self-Awareness) and walking in authentic Self-Alignment—at work and at home—through our choices to live the kind of lives that matter to us. In my experience, Self-Trust is a powerful path to a world where people can disagree and still respect one another.

No matter how much I play out every worst case scenario in my head, the truth is this: I have a 100 percent survival rate of the worst days of my life. And so do you. In fact, when I found myself earlier this spring in an actual traumatic emergency—when I rushed Eli to the ER by ambulance and they ended up admitting him for three days—I realized I will *always* do whatever needs to be done in an actual emergency.

When my Head stops overthinking and my Heart freezes in fear, my Belly Wisdom—my instincts as a mother, my intuition—kicks in like a generator. I just need to remember to let go of the anxious thoughts that spiral during tough times and have enough Self-Trust in myself that I *will* meet that challenge with courage and hope—because I already did.

The path to cultivating authentic Self-Trust includes three key Wayfinding signposts: befriending your Inner Critic, practicing equanimity, and building and maintaining boundaries. These signposts fall under the ability to discriminate between thoughts motivated by fear and thoughts motivated by strength. Here is where we shift from Head and Heart knowledge to our Belly Wisdom.

One of the goals of personal evolution is to still our fear enough that we can make intentional Wayfinding choices. The reward is being able to truly have peace, knowing that we can trust life's timing even when things do not work out the way we want them to. We can have an awareness and be fully present in the moment and trust that all things begin—and end—just as they are meant to.

BEFRIEND YOUR INNER CRITIC

My friend Trenton Sweet, author of *Awakening the Tranquil Warrior*, once reminded me that the way we treat others reflects how we treat ourselves. His comment made me think about the time I was given feedback by one of my coaches (right before she quit) that I was a terrible boss because my expectations were unrealistic. I remember being shocked at this. After all, I didn't expect anything from her that I didn't expect of myself, right? In my peer mentoring cohorts, we always have "no judgment" as a part of our guiding principles. But in my decades of group coaching thousands of people, I have rarely seen one participant judge another. But what I do see in every session with every company on every continent I have worked is people judging themselves—over and over and over again.

I do not like the term Imposter Syndrome for far too many reasons to count here. But I think we can all agree that there is a critical voice in our Heads guided, as we have learned, by our belief systems. I call the voice my Inner Critic. Here's what is important to remember if you *hear* the voice: You *aren't* the voice.

Think about that for a minute.

If that is true—and I believe it is—then like any other voice that offers you advice or feedback, you can simply choose to listen to it or not.

The trouble is that when we lose touch with our inner knowing—the whisper in our Belly that knows our truth and always sees the next step forward—our Inner Critic gets louder and louder, judging all we think and do.

Allow me to introduce you to my Inner Critic. She's quite stern with her thin, white hair severely pulled back in a tight chignon. Her face is lined, and if you give her half a second, she will tell you that she's seen it all—multiple times over. Her mouth is pursed tightly, and with her arms tucked across her chest, she whispers to me, eyebrows pinched, "You're not good enough."

I call her Edith.

As an entrepreneur, I am always looking for opportunities to grow and share the best practices I've learned about what works—what really works—in leadership and life. I'm curious if your company is investing in taking care of their people, and why or why not. I want to know if retaining GenZ is a topic of debate in your meetings. I will likely ask if you know of any organizations who want to improve the mental health and well-being of their employees or improve their culture. I have a hundred questions.

But when I have these conversations, Edith stalks up behind me, dressed for her role as judge. Her breath is hot on the back of my neck, her long black robes pooling around a starched white dickey so bright it hurts my eyes.

"You ask too much."

"Quit being so self-promoting."

"You look obnoxious."

I recall a time nearly a decade ago now when she said, "You don't belong here."

That particular line came as I was in a regional community meeting of C-Suite leaders in my hometown of Pittsburgh. At thirty-seven, I was the youngest in the room by far. I was also one of only three people who were self-employed. As I looked at the corporate powerhouses seated around the table, my stomach began to churn. The chair began the meeting, and as the pace picked up, so did my anxious thoughts spiral.

What can I contribute? What insight would even be relevant?
Should I say something? If I do, what will they think?
What if they think I am being—gasp—self-promoting?
What will they think if I say nothing at all?

With Edith's hand tightly clasped over my mouth, I silently listened as a question about engaging and developing young people went answered. The conversation started to turn in a direction that my intuition told me was not the best course of action, but I held back because of the fear that someone, maybe, possibly, kinda-sorta could judge me as self-promoting. Self-serving. Selfish.

Finally, in the midst of my internal debate with my not-invisible-enough-foe, I heard my own voice and the clear tenor of my knowledge and enthusiasm ring out, because if there is one thing that overrides Edith and her haughty demeanor, it's my passion about personal development in the professional world. Yes, just as we were about to move to the next topic, I found my voice.

Deep down, deeper and stronger than Edith, I knew that the insight I had to offer was aligned with my business. After all, my insight is directly correlated with my expertise. It's what I know and what I do. And I also knew that what I had to say was the right feedback to share.

As I offered my opinion to those powerhouse leaders, I realized for the first time that I didn't sneak in the back of the room and find a seat at the table. I was invited there. And I was invited there for my voice, so I best use it.

My friends, we fear judgment from others because most of us live with it echoing inside our heads. And when we judge other people—which we *all* do—the aspects we focus on are often mirrors for the parts of ourselves we do not like. We judge others for their parenting, or lack of, when we feel insecure in our own parenting journey. We judge our next door neighbor's marriage because we fear for ours. But when we stop fearing the truth about ourselves, the truth becomes our guide.

PRACTICE EQUANIMITY

I truly believe that our biggest fear is not death or public speaking, no matter what social media may say. It is being judged for who we actually are beneath the masks and the armor. Our greatest fear is taking the risk to be fully alive and express who we really are. As we have learned while moving through the self-limiting beliefs of Self-Awareness and shifting our choices with intention of Self-Alignment, the gift of Self-Trust is beginning to know and genuinely like ourselves. We understand how we have built walls, some even in our own minds, to protect ourselves, learning to live our lives by trying to satisfy the demands of others. From parents and coaches to teachers and church leaders, we prioritize what others want from us and learn to align our actions accordingly.

As we grow up, we add our partners and bosses, and even our children as voices we fear will judge our choices. And as we Wayfind through life, we have an inherent fear of not being accepted, of not being truly good enough for someone else, of not belonging. And so we create an image of what we "should be." Our minds craft an image of what perfection looks like based on what others have told us.

But because perfection does not exist in the human condition, we ultimately fail to live up to that image, an image *we* created, by the way. And since we have internalized the self-limiting belief that only perfection is "good," when we do not meet it, we assume we are "bad." And so we reject ourselves. We judge ourselves. We harm ourselves. And oh, how we suffer.

Emotional self-harm is a beast to unlearn. As I was on my personal evolution journey these last few years, I realized that I chose to stay down and out as a punishment. I am embarrassed to say this, but it was to teach myself a lesson. Because of my self-limiting beliefs, I believed I wasn't worthy of comfort or ease. I wasn't worthy of wealth. Success. Love.

And nearly all my suffering was self-inflicted because I lacked Self-Worth. I led my life desperately trying to fill my heart through external validation such as awards, accolades, social media "likes," best-seller statuses, and published articles—and also through unhealthy codependent relationships at work and at home. I set up my life ensuring that I was "needed." Never giving myself permission to receive help ensured that my Vitality Voltage was drained across the board.

Self-Trust is the ability to, as consistently as possible, practice equanimity, the art of feeling our feelings without getting carried away with them. It is intentional (and thoughtful) energy management, incorporating rest and recovery into our weeks and our days. It is understanding what depletes, drains, and recharges our energy and having the ability to deftly manage it with intention. It is making amends to yourself and showing up for yourself in the ways that matter to you, right now. Just as trust is built between people consistently, slowly over time, so is Self-Trust.

Equanimity also comes from learning how to discern what is yours and what is not. When we hold onto things that don't belong to us, it disrupts our batteries emotionally and, in my experience, physically. Here's the truth, my friends. We cannot hate ourselves into becoming better versions of ourselves. We can only love ourselves to evolution. The only path home to ourselves is the one that requires us to intentionally choose *not* to belittle, blame, or shame ourselves. This is the space where we practice Self-Trust.

Cultivating equanimity through emotional rest includes giving ourselves permission to literally be a mess. Remember the caterpillar analogy? Self-Trust is learning and embodying that it's okay to *not* be okay sometimes. And it is *also* okay to be okay, even when those I love are not. And of course, it is okay to be okay even when life around us is not. Without equanimity and emotional rest, personal evolution becomes a to-do list. Wayfinding done well is choosing to begin exactly where we are in life. And it is both liberating and gracious to ourselves.

That's why the Year of Me was so life-changing for me. After more than four decades of prioritizing others, it was almost shocking to ask myself at my morning ritual every morning,

"What do *I* most want out of this day? How can I look for ways to delight myself?"

Sometimes the answer is carving out time to work without the distraction of email to focus on a project. Other days it means treating myself to an ice cream cone on the way home from the grocery store—even before dinner—something I swore to myself as a little girl I would do every chance I got.

Instead of waiting for our partners, our children, or our bosses to make us happy, what if we intentionally found ways to make ourselves happy every day?

It is absolutely something we all have the power to do … if we choose.

BUILD AND MAINTAIN BOUNDARIES WITH YOURSELF

The third key aspect of practicing Self-Trust is giving yourself permission to create boundaries. We cannot talk about Self-Trust and not talk about boundaries. Authentic Self-Trust is no longer self-abandoning under the guise of taking care of others. Self-Trust includes the art of setting and sustaining boundaries with others, but mostly with ourselves. While many of us have self-limiting beliefs about boundaries, boundaries are really quite simple. We just have to ask ourselves, "What is okay?" and "What isn't okay?"

As we build and maintain boundaries with ourselves in our lives, the important areas to focus on internally are boundaries that align with our Vitality Voltage. What charges your batteries, and what boundaries do you need to put in place to ensure that you can power up by incorporating intentional periods of rest and recovery into your whole life—at work and at home?

Often we break promises to ourselves. We promise ourselves we will leave work on time, go to the gym, and prioritize physical rest. But then we find so many excuses to break those promises. It wasn't until I had both a physical and mental health crisis that I finally stopped making excuses and actively kept my promises. And my Self-Trust grew.

We need to set boundaries in our minds to silence our Inner Critic. We need to choose our thoughts with intention and not allow outdated self-limiting beliefs to set our agenda, as we learned in Self-Awareness and Self-Alignment. These boundaries allow us to practice equanimity, the art of feeling our emotions without being overtaken by them. In fact, the ability to recognize, create, and maintain healthy boundaries allows me to stay out of enmeshment with the emotions of others.

As I've said, Self-Trust is the spot on my Wayfinding Compass that I struggle with the most. In my nearly three decades of coaching, I've discovered that the boundaries I break most often are the boundaries I set with myself. I know what I need to do, but I don't do it.

I especially have difficulty setting and maintaining emotional boundaries within myself. I find myself wanting to take responsibility for the emotions and actions of others, sacrificing myself by ignoring my physical, mental, emotional, and spiritual needs, and numbing out the inevitable discomforts.

Here's what I really want you to know. If any of this resonates with you, it is *not* your fault.

My friends, we were all taught to be this way. It was modeled by those who came before us. It was praised and rewarded in our schools, churches, communities, and cultures. But here is the thing: If you want to live a more fulfilled life, if you want to successfully Wayfind through your personal evolution right now— at work or at home— you have to do the work of forging a new path ahead. This is the path to Wayfinding joy in your life again.

Once I realized that every time I prioritized someone else's needs my own got back burnered, I realized that this model of living was unsustainable—that every *yes* to someone else was a *no* of some sort to me.

I am not suggesting that you say *yes* to yourself more than you say *yes* to others. Just begin with equity. For every *yes* to someone, offer a *yes* to yourself. Simply match it.

For example, if Kevin asks me to attend a big event with his extended family, I can match that *yes* with time at the pool by myself this weekend with my favorite book to recharge my battery. If a teammate at work had an emergency on Tuesday night and I worked two hours later than expected, I can balance that *yes* by starting later on Wednesday morning and attending a Pilates class.

For a *yes* that drains you, say *yes* to something that recharges you. As adults, we have to remember that no one else is in charge of taking care of you but you.

Self-Trust is consistently practicing rest and recovery cycles, giving ourselves permission to plug into what recharges us (at a minimum weekly and ideally daily), and knowing that we deserve a full night's sleep, a good walk outside, or in my case, a Pilates class in the middle of the workday to clear my mind and charge my mental battery. It is being content at work, eating nourishing foods, and not just giving but receiving.

Self-Trust is knowing that we are worthy of being loved and loving others, just as we are. A mentor of mine once said to me that the road to hell is paved by small acts of self-betrayal. If that is true, then I would say that the road to Self-Trust is paved by small promises made to yourself that you have consistently honored. The road to self-liberation is paved by small acts of surrender to our own inner knowing. And the road toward the next point on our Wayfinding Compass—Self-Worth—is paved by integration and embodiment. This is where we practice the skill of bringing in all the abandoned aspects of ourselves as we journey back home to ourselves.

6

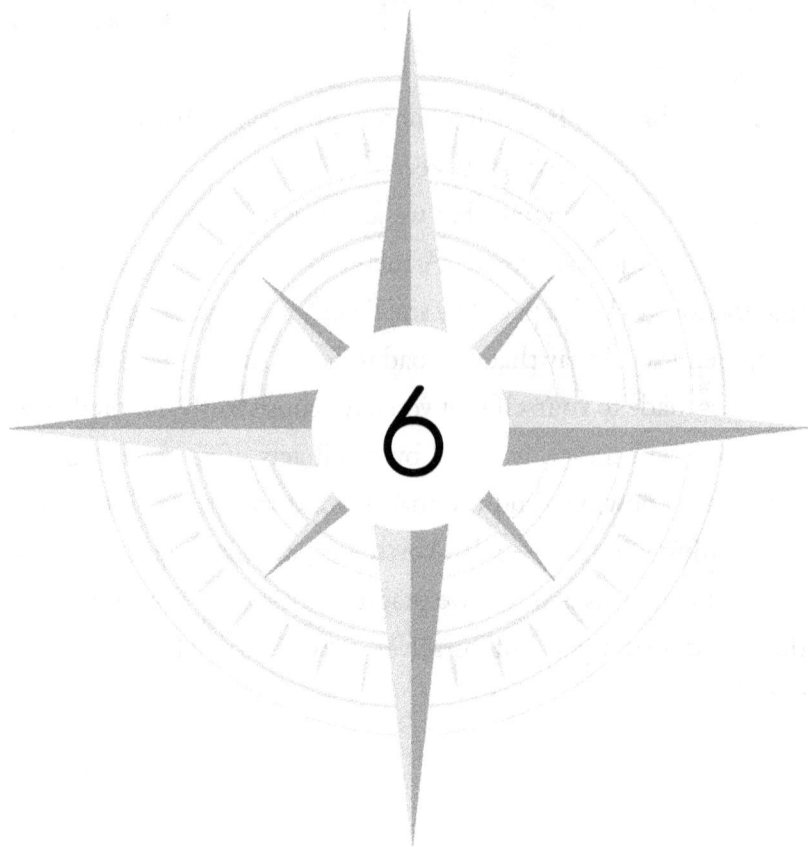

SELF-WORTH
Reprogramming Your
Belief Systems

Author and speaker Cory Muscara said, "There is no amount of 'fixing yourself' that could possibly make you more whole than you are right now."[10] This concept rocked my world. Sit with that for a moment. You are already whole. You never have been broken.

You cannot *be* broken.

My friends, wholeness is not something you achieve; it's something you remember. And that involves connecting to that healthy feminine energy. It involves the very real leadership and life skill of surrender. Of acceptance. Of forgiveness.

There are literally scores of research in our post-pandemic world around the crisis of mental health and well-being inside of organizations. CEOs are spending millions upon millions of dollars on Employee Assistance Programs (EAPs) that are woefully underutilized—to the tune of a 1–3 percent utilization rate—even in highly engaged cultures. Why? Why aren't people leveraging these amazing resources to support their well-being?

Why aren't you?

Here's why I didn't. It was because we cannot manage well-being and Self-Worth through an app or an EAP. The time has come to shift the conversation about mental health and well-being from an individual challenge to a collective experience. We need a new model. We need an evolution to our outdated, collective belief system about what defines mental health. And it starts with Self-Awareness, Self-Alignment, and Self-Trust. And it wouldn't be complete without Self-Worth.

Compared to previous generations, most of the companies and communities where we live, work, and play are missing spaces of vulnerability, empathy, and co-regulation. How do we heal a toxic culture?

We do it by helping one person at a time. Everyone is worthy of help. In my space of the workplace, that means not just the executives and not just the high-potentials. The middle matters.

When I started EDGE Leadership, I used to hide the fact that our focus was personal development in a professional setting. I worried that people wouldn't take me seriously, that companies wouldn't pay for development about resetting self-limiting belief systems, shifting self-sabotaging behaviors, or building Self-Trust and resilience. And that if they did, they would only be willing to do so for the employees their company's (woefully outdated) nine-box calibration grids told them had high potential, the ones they deemed worthy of that investment.

No more. After Wayfinding through my own personal evolution journey across my Growth Mountains, I know deep in my own Belly Wisdom that *everyone* has potential. And so we have evolved from an executive and leadership development coaching and consulting company to one that helps companies engage the middle 80 percent of their talent by focusing on mental health, personal well-being, and professional growth.

Now we get to work with the average folks like me who are disengaged, unhappy, and lacking Self-Awareness and Self-Alignment, who have little to no Self-Trust and Self-Worth. That is important because how can we be expected to do our best work when we are far from our best self? Truthfully, we can't.

More than the other cardinal directions on our Wayfinding Compass, West (Self-Worth) is very much a posture of receiving, of surrender. There isn't the same masculine "muscling" that we often find in the intense curiosity of the North (Self-Awareness) or the robustness of the action orientation of the East (Self-Alignment). In the West is the sunset, the final warm rays of the sun at the end of a long, fulfilling day.

Here's what I know for sure about the art of receiving. It brings peace. And it has two distinct signposts. Peace takes courageous, decisive action, and it requires open hands to receive it. Authentic peace requires hope—hope that in all things, no matter what, I *will always* show up for myself. And every time I honor my Wantings, I am proving that I can be counted on to be dependable to myself. I will not under any circumstance let the "little girl" inside me down. Self-Worth is a space of radical acceptance of what is, underpinned with self-love and self-compassion. It is ensuring that I am my own priority—every day.

The path to Self-Worth is the *who* of our Wayfinding Compass. Who I am is built slowly over time through the *when*, the consistent acts of Self-Trust. If you think about it, isn't that how the bonds between two people build? I fell in love with Kevin because he showed up for me, proving he was dependable. He knew what I wanted and went out of his way to provide it to me. As humans, we can only trust others (or the Universe) to the degree to which we trust ourselves. Self-Worth is built from showing up for yourself as much as you show up for everyone else. And we can only show up for ourselves when we know who we are, what we want (Self-Awareness), and how to align our choices intentionally every day (Self-Alignment).

One of the biggest revelations I had in the last few years is the fact that everything in my inner world is reflected in my outer world. As Michelle Buczkowski said in her Foreword to this book, I realized that the world was not coming at me but that I was coming at the world.

Self-Worth has both an inward and an outward aspect. It involves holding the tension between a deep relationship within ourselves and the awareness of the behaviors, choices, thoughts, and actions that shape our feelings. Self-Alignment of both our interior *and* our exterior (not either/or) is what ultimately guides our Wayfinding path back home to ourselves.

As we cultivate our Self-Worth, there are three best practices to maximize this point on our Wayfinding Compass. The first is reprogramming our belief systems now that we have identified our self-limiting beliefs and seen firsthand the impact they have on our lives. Next is maintaining hope, trusting that even unscheduled events that interrupt our lives are a form of divine direction. Lastly, the path to Self-Worth includes being able to accept all, eliminating expectations and our desire to understand *why* at every turn. When done well, Self-Worth brings peace. And I promise you, that alone is worth the effort.

REPROGRAM YOUR BELIEF SYSTEM AND TRANSFORM YOUR PERSONAL POWER

Our belief systems are illusions—powerful ones but illusions nonetheless. It is our belief in them that makes them reality for us. And here's the thing. Because we are the ones who make the belief system real, we can at any point in our life decide to change them. For example, as I stated in the opening of this book, if we believe that the world is a place of suffering, that will define our reality. But we can choose to believe the opposite, that the world is a place of hope. Changing what we focus on in life changes what we see. Wayfinding is less about discovering new lands and more about creating new eyes to see.

Connecting to our intuition—our Belly Wisdom—is the natural outcome of building our Self-Worth. As I have found in my own healing journey, both physically and mentally, our bodies thrive when our spirits thrive. When our truest, most authentic self takes charge of reprogramming our belief system, our physical environment literally shifts to accommodate.

Over the last decade of my life, I have worked with coaches, therapists, and healers around reprogramming my belief system, and the last two years specifically on the self-limiting belief that taking care of myself is selfish. Whew! That one was heavy. Based on what I discovered in Self-Alignment, I struggled with maintaining boundaries with myself about going to the gym three days a week, making time to stop work, and eating a nutritious lunch. I realized that my sense of worth was tied to my need to bring value. I feared that if I didn't do enough for others, then ultimately they wouldn't love me.

⊕ FIELD NOTES

Below I will share the self-coaching process from a mentor of mine that I followed in the hopes that you can leverage it as well. You will see that each step has a fill in the blank. Try not to overthink it, and then let your answers come from your Belly and not your Head. I included my own vulnerable responses so you can see how it worked for me.

1. **What am I most afraid of? (Think of the first fear that pops up and don't judge it.)**

   If I _____ , I worry that _____ .

   If I truly prioritize myself over others, I worry that I will lose people. I will be alone.

2. **Further redefine my limiting belief.**

   If I _____ , then _____ .

   If I choose myself first, then I will live a life alone.

3. **Reframe the possibility.**

   When I _____ , then _____ .

   When I choose myself, then the right people will choose me.

4. **Identify and understand the energy and emotion underneath the words.**

    When I feel a sense of ⬚ , what do I need to feel whole?

    When I feel a sense of abandonment, what do I need to feel whole?

5. **How can I best give that to myself? What do I want?**

    What do I need to feel whole when I am feeling ⬚ ?

    What do I need to feel whole when I am feeling abandoned?

    Some examples for me:

    *   Release unwanted energy from my body through movement and activity
    *   Choose my thoughts with intention (redirect my anxiety spiral and rumination pattern)
    *   Cry
    *   Reconnect to my Belly Wisdom through meditation or prayer
    *   Spend time with Kevin
    *   Find solitude (especially in nature)
    *   Journal

MAINTAIN EVERYDAY HOPE

A mentor once told me that wisdom = life experiences + the ability to detach. Contrary to popular belief, detachment is not apathy or lack of interest. Healthy detachment is the ability to quiet your fear-driving Inner Critic and the corresponding self-limiting belief systems. It comes from Self-Trust, having faith in yourself, and knowing that everything is unfolding as it is meant to and that no matter what, you can and will come out better in the end.

As we move across our Wayfinding Compass between the West (Self-Worth) and the North (Self-Awareness), we see how beautifully they are connected. As we have been through the darkness, now we can see the light. Self-Worth is where we maintain our core values from Self-Awareness and walk in alignment with them consistently. It is believing that you have everything you need to climb the Growth Mountain ahead of you.

And the one after that.

And the one after that too.

You are enough right now, just as you are. And when you may need more, like when they were rushing my son to the ER, you *will* find it, right on time. And you always have. That, my friends, is the power of Self-Trust.

Everyday hope is living a life of gratitude, a concept that has been written about in every culture in every generation in the history of the world because it's so deeply essential to the human spirit. One thing I have discovered during my Wayfinding journey is that practicing gratitude is less of a doing (the masculine power center) and more of a being (the feminine power center). When we express gratitude for what we have, even in the waves of anxiety, fear, grief, and sadness, we learn to cope a little better, and we find that we can hang in there a little longer.

Gratitude and everyday hope are being present in the pain and the duality of life. Once again, like everything in our Wayfinding Compass, it exists in the tension between. It is both/and, not either/or. It is not black and white. Wayfinding is what happens in the middle. And the middle is messy. Personal Evolution is fluid in one moment, choppy in the next. It's liberating, expansive, intuitive, complicated, and transformative. And yet it is so, so worthwhile.

Gratitude is also not just about what we can offer to others or being grateful for the gifts we receive. Most of us struggle to truly appreciate ourselves. I ignored myself for decades of my adult life—committed to everyone and everything else—and never once offered myself the gift of gratitude. Until my Wayfinding journey across my Personal Growth Mountain, I never saw my own human beauty and truly honored my gifts and my strengths, not more than but just as much as my flaws and mistakes. Cultivating sustainable Self-Worth is holding space for both at the same time.

ACCEPT ALL

Only when we establish a consciousness of appreciation can we tackle the challenge of forgiving ourselves for being our own worst enemy. Despite the atrocities we have experienced in our lives and all the abuse and pain, for most of us, the majority of the shame we feel comes from within. Just as there is peace that comes from forgiving others, there is peace to be found in forgiving ourselves, to know deep in our Hearts and our Bellies that we did the best we could with what we had at the time. With the dependability built from sustained Self-Trust comes the promise that now that we know better, we *will* do better for our future selves, our current selves, and the inner child who still lives inside us.

To accept is to be present, to be fully in the body and not caught up in our thoughts and feelings. It is to remember that while our brain can only process 40 bits of information per second, but our bodies can process 11 *million.*

Our body is designed to protect us across our Wayfinding journeys in life. We feel cold, so we put on another layer of clothing. We feel thirsty when we need hydration, so we drink some water. Our bodies don't care if someone is thinner than we are or has more money. Its needs are more base—almost animalistic in a way.

◈ FIELD NOTES

Humans are the only animals (that we know of anyway) that punish themselves for making the same mistake more than once. I can't even count how many times I have punished myself for the same mistakes—at work and at home. I invite you to think about that for a minute.

Consider the last *big* mistake you made at work. At home. What did you do? What did you learn from it?
How many times did you punish yourself for this mistake?
How are you punishing yourself still?
What would it look like to let it go, to bless the experience for what it has taught you, and then release it?

The friendly squirrel who lives in my backyard doesn't care if his neighbor has more nuts, and he doesn't beat himself up for not having more. The squirrel just continues his search for enough food, just what his body needs.

In the same way, once I built a trusting relationship with my body, it has become my most useful asset. It can—in a moment— offer me effective decision-making, access my creativity, and identify my essential needs. And I only need to ask myself, "What do I need next? What do I want?"

When I can ask those questions from a quiet, grounded space, the right next step is whispered to me from deep in my Belly. My friends, the answers you need are *always* within you. You only need to trust yourself enough to ask and love yourself enough to listen.

Acceptance also involves the skill of letting go. We must let go first of what does not serve us in order to have space in our hands to receive what does. Letting go is hard, but what if it is the only way to make room for something greater?

There is a powerful activity I sometimes do with my coaching clients, called My Releasing Jar. I encourage them to fill it with any self-limiting beliefs they want to let go of, any unhelpful comments from their Inner Critic, mistakes they made that cause them shame, or even anxious thoughts they struggle with.

To make your own, grab a container of some sort. I chose a simple Mason jar that I keep beside my desk at work. Place small pieces of paper or, in my case, a stack of sticky notes next to the jar. When you're ready, write "I am letting go of" and then fill in whatever pops into your mind.

Go ahead and try it. Here are a few I am letting go of that are sitting in my jar right now.

▶ I have to to have my sh** together all the time.

▶ The need to be perfect.

▶ Places where I am just tolerated and not celebrated.

▶ The hurtful response I said to Kevin last week.

Keep the jar somewhere visible with paper and pens beside it. Whenever you catch yourself in an old pattern of self-blame and guilt, write down what you need to let go of and place it in your Releasing Jar.

You may repeat some of the things many times. And that is okay. There is no right or wrong way to do this. Notice how it feels to let go of the bad that you perceive about yourself and what space it creates for the good—how it feels to let the old go with hope for the new.

Doing this allows you to stretch your new muscles of Self-Trust and Self-Worth by funneling your new energy that you are gaining from your rest and recovery cycles, and practicing the new skill of self-compassion. Letting go is hard, hard work. Few of us were taught or shown how to do it. Many of us watch our parents, grandparents, aunties, and uncles even today still beating themselves up for a comment they said many years ago or a choice they made decades ago.

The letting go that leads to acceptance and Self-Worth takes self-compassion, patience, and energy, and requires a fully charged Vitality Voltage. Remember that our brains are pattern-making machines and that the science of neuroplasticity tells us that practice via repetition is the path to growth. And dare I say, letting go allows our hearts to grow too.

Learning to let go of the self-limiting belief that "maintaining control keeps me safe" was a huge step on my Wayfinding journey toward personal evolution and remembering my authentic sense of Self-Worth. I used to believe that the more I controlled a situation, the safer I would be. After all, I had imagined every possible scenario, right? Nothing could sneak up on me until I found myself in an ambulance with Eli, thinking my kid was going to die right in front of me.

Holding onto that self-limiting belief that worry=control kept me trapped. Yes, I thought through 876 possible scenarios, but I had only thought of the *bad* ones, the worst scenarios. And each one fed my anxious thoughts more. How could my life have changed at work and at home if I'd spent even 25 percent of the time envisioning the good or the truly amazing possibilities instead of just all the bad ones?

When we live in the past (the "could haves" or "should haves") or the future (the "if/thens"), we miss the beauty of the present.

Trust the Wayfinding process. I have personally tested this work with thousands of people just like you. Our team of coaches have shared it with tens of thousands. Most of all, trust yourself.

When we accept, we naturally release our doubts. It is the ultimate posture of receiving. It is meeting ourselves exactly where we are at this moment and letting that be enough—over and over.

Again and again.

Forever.

There is so much power and momentum in acknowledging our Self-Worth. All will be well. We hate feeling powerless. But here's what I learned through my own personal evolution: What if we are actually power*ful*—not less? What if we already have all the power we need? In my life, it means accepting that even though I was an imperfect mother, what if I did for my kid exactly what I needed to in his childhood, and now I am a companion (and hopefully an occasional Mountain Guide) on his journey?

Being present also involves the ability of following our Wantings. We first talked about the importance of knowing what we want through Self-Awareness and discussed how to follow what we truly want in our lives. As we find ourselves deeper in our Wayfinding journeys, we must employ our Heads, Hearts, *and* Bellies in the exploration.

As we do this well as leaders, our direct reports and our peers will watch and learn. When we do this well as partners, parents, siblings, and friends, we unconsciously give permission to those around us to do the same—within and without. The micro affects the macro. This is how we change the world—by changing ourselves.

Different seasons in our lives will require different types of Wayfinding, and all seasons must be punctuated by periods of rest and recovery from an energy standpoint. I believe that personal evolution is the ultimate human quest. We keep coming back to the same places with new eyes. As we go, we must remember that we need peers, companions, and an occasional wise Mountain Guide along the way because maps of new lands are never built alone.

7

DON'T GO IT ALONE
The Value of Third Places
and Peer Groups

I have been asked many times how you know if you are ready for personal evolution. I have found that there are three signposts to watch for. If you have two or more, then it's probably time to pack your bags. The first is an absence of meaning and purpose. There may be an inherent tugging in your Belly that something is out of alignment. Like my earlier caterpillar analogy, you're not who you once were, so what once brought you meaning no longer does.

You know you are here when you feel a deep longing that you can't quite put your finger on. For me, I learned about this signpost when I tried (unsuccessfully) to alleviate my lack of meaning or purpose by shuffling around the external components of my life. I had a baby, I got divorced, I got a new job.

The second signpost is increased anxiety. Like I shared earlier, reframing anxiety means seeing it not only as a mental diagnosis or disorder and securing support from a medical professional as I did, but also as alarm bells that something in our life is out of alignment. For me, it was a loss of self-identity. A lack of Self-Awareness. Zero Self-Alignment and Self-Trust. I was no longer sure of who I was and what I wanted out of life. Not only did I not like myself, I actively *disliked* myself.

The third signpost is a deep desire for connection with others, what I call a lack of hope. Caroline Myss, an author and teacher, explained in her book *Anatomy of the Spirit* that with this kind of psychological crisis we recognize that we are the cause and that our unhappiness is not coming from others around us.[11] Before I could begin my Wayfinding journey in earnest, I had to own that the cause of my suffering was within me and not my external life components. I discovered that the inadequacy of the external components of my life was a *consequence* of my personal evolution crisis, *not* the cause. At that point, it was time to face my greatest fear.

As I've said, contrary to popular belief, humanity's biggest fear is not public speaking or even death. I believe our biggest fear is to be Seen—with a capital S—Seen for who we really are and not who we project, perform, or try to perfect. For me, this was embracing the power of vulnerability, taking the risk to be alive and express who I am with all my imperfections, all my mistakes, and all my humanness. Many of us have learned to live our lives trying to satisfy the demands of those around us. And that is why very few of us have curated an innate sense of Self-Worth.

When we lack worthiness, we do not take care of ourselves. And when we don't take care of ourselves, we do not have the capacity to care for others—at work or at home. We cannot do our best work when we are not in alignment with our best self. So how do we connect back home to ourselves again?

Have you ever stopped to wonder why there is such an epidemic of mental health and well-being in today's world, both at work with our teams and at home in our lives?

Part of it—to be sure—is science. We have the ability to diagnose medical health in ways we never could before. Part of it is technology. We have gathered a lot of data about the impact of our phones and how they disrupt our natural dopamine cycles.

We are more connected than ever before in the history of the world and yet more disconnected than we have ever been. Thankfully, important conversations are happening about connection, belonging, and mental health. As I have moved through my personal evolution these last few years, I believe another reason we are struggling with human connection has to do with the concept of the Three Places. Based on the work of sociologist Ray Oldenburg in *The Great Good Place*, there is fascinating research around what humans need in order to thrive, and that is having access to our three specific spaces: Home (First Place), Work (Second Place), and Community (Third Place).

1st Place	2nd Place	3rd Place
🏠	🖥️	👥

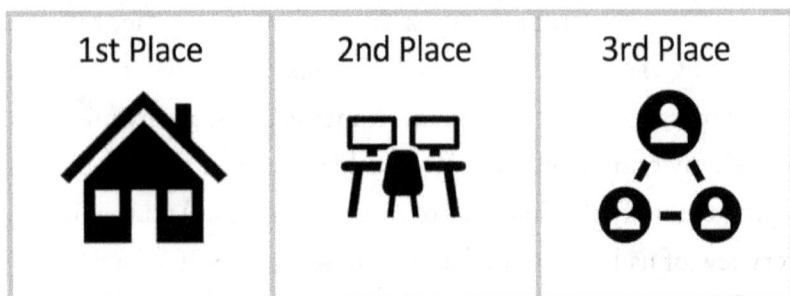

For me, when numbing out and avoiding just wasn't enough to cope with my mental health anymore, I started digging deep into leading edge research around nervous system regulation and energy management. I began working with teachers, life coaches, and healers about how to identify self-limiting belief systems and triggers, how to build back my Self-Trust and cultivate authentic Self-Worth. Basically, I wanted to know how to love myself again.

So I started researching what human beings have always needed to thrive across generations and continents, through wars and famines. One thing kept bubbling up: Community. Community is what Ray Oldenburg called a Third Place. His research states that for optimal well-being, humans need access to three specific places, not just to survive but to thrive.

Let's start with what he refers to as our First Place: Home. This is what many of us refer to as our personal life. It is the space that encompasses our immediate family. Our First Place has roles: I am a mother, a wife, a daughter, an aunt. And as we have already learned, whenever we have a role to play, we also have expectations that go along with them. And with expectations, we also have judgments and self-limiting beliefs. These are often invisible, internal checklists of what we believe makes a good mom, a good wife, a good daughter, and so on. And usually these checklists are underpinned by our self-limiting beliefs.

Our Second Place, Work, has a lot in common with our First Place, Home. Work is where we make our living. Once again, it is a space defined by roles. I am a CEO, a leader, a Coach, a vendor partner, a teammate. And where there are roles, there are expectations and judgments to determine if we are succeeding or failing based on those invisible checklists of what makes us "good."

As Oldenburg explains, our Third Place is very different. This space is not at all like our First or Second Places. The Third Place is less a specific location but instead represents Community. Unlike the structured spaces of Home and Work, the Third Place is a space that has no set role for us to play. It is simply where we can show up exactly how we are on any given day. It serves as a brave space where we can lean into vulnerability about where we are struggling in our First and Second Places.

Third Places are defined by two primary criteria: vulnerability and consistency. Vulnerability is so we can talk openly about our challenges and celebrate our successes. Consistency is so our peers know what is going on in our homes and at work and genuinely want to know how we are feeling.

Third Places meet consistently enough to know what's going on in each other's lives, at a minimum monthly but ideally weekly or even biweekly. It is where people can ask me, "I know Eli has finals this week. How is he doing?" or "I know you are in the throes of editing the new book. What are you really loving about it so far?" Third Places call us forth as mirrors to truly know ourselves (Self-Awareness), unlock our personal power, and hold us accountable

(Self-Alignment) to change our behaviors in the ways that matter most to us. Third Places are active spaces of co-regulation, and they build Self-Trust.

This space of a Community of peers is essential to raising our personal consciousness and Wayfind successfully through personal evolution. Third Places create the growth container where we can actively challenge and change the rules we live by at work and at home. They do so by helping us rewrite and often reprogram the belief systems we maintain. They challenge us to ask what success means to us today for who I am right now.

What if a successful life isn't defined by achieving what society tells us are the "right" goals, status, or job title? How would our lives change if success is no longer defined by our outdated belief systems but instead defined by our ability to self-regulate, and the capacity to work through the challenges that will always pop up along our Wayfinding journeys? As we raise our personal consciousness as individuals, we raise the collective because vulnerability begets vulnerability, and rising tides lift all boats together.

Third Places are active spaces that inspire self-compassion and empathy. They are spaces where we can be both fully seen and heard, where we know that we belong—just as we are.

According to Oldenburg's research on what we need to thrive, which of the Three Places do you think was the largest historically? Consider that until very recently in history, humans lived in tribes, clans, villages, or multigenerational homes where grandparents and even great-grandparents lived together with their children and grandchildren. We nursed each other's babies, and people cared for each other's needs. This was Community.

Historically...

Even around the beginning of the twentieth century, homes didn't all have a telephone. Folks would go down the street to a physical Third Place that served as the hub of the neighborhood such as the corner store or the local pub. Community was literally the air we breathed.

Oldenburg's research was focused on post–Industrial Revolution communities, and he was super curious about the post–World War II rise of the suburbs that began a steady disintegration of our physical Third Places. After World War II, people moved out to new suburbs, traveling to work in city centers in their cars. And coming home at the end of the day, they may have passed a neighbor or two on their street and waved as they drove by. But then they turned, headed down the driveway and into their garage, popped up inside their house, and never spoke to another human soul. Over the last thirty years, technology has exacerbated this as televisions filled our First Places and we no longer needed to leave home to get the news anymore.

As technology advanced and the Internet emerged, the importance and focus on our First and Second Places began to grow larger and larger, silently absconding the space that the Third Place once occupied. Even attending movie theaters in the Community began to diminish as streaming services allowed us to get our entertainment at home. Our Second Place began its rapid climb with the advent of the knowledge workforce, and technology created the opportunity for work to literally follow us home.

And so it did, once again at the cost of our Third Place.

For generations of us across America, the most common Third Place was the church. Organized religion was a traditional space in the post-industrial world, incorporating communities of peers on a weekly basis, separate from work and home. People didn't need to play a role (unless they actively chose one) and as such were released from the automatic tethers of expectation and judgment. Most church communities were spaces of vulnerability and belonging when done well. And yet in recent years, for a whole host of reasons, attendance at churches has declined.

Last 30 Years...

As our Third Places were diminishing at a more rapid pace than ever before in human history and our Second Place (Work) began taking up more and more of our waking hours—including traditional periods of rest and recovery—the increased focus on our First Place became a pressure cooker. People began to see their Vitality Voltage drain as the expectations of those pesky roles in their personal lives started growing larger and all-consuming.

We used to only compare ourselves to family, friends, and the people next door, but then our connections grew to encompass millions of people. Before the Internet, our circles and hence our comparisons and judgments were limited to people we knew in person. Now we can compare ourselves to masses of people we will never meet in real life whom we only know through carefully curated images and snapshots of their lives.

Community, our Third Place, has diminished even further as online comparison has stolen our time, happiness, and sense of belonging. Most of us didn't realize the extent of our Third Place's disintegration until 2020 when all of the sudden our First and Second Places became one. For the first time for the majority of people in every country and every continent in the world, home and work occupied the exact same space during the COVID lockdowns. And people freaked out.

Pandemic...

Without any separation between our two primary places (home and work), we were faced with loneliness to a degree never fully experienced or acknowledged before. For the vast majority of us, it was the first time in our lives we saw that we were missing our Third Place. There was no avoiding it or ignoring it.

Companies and executives shifted the blame on the pandemic and remote work, but I believe that is a red herring. I believe we are finally feeling the loss of our Third Place. And even for the very few folks who realized that they had little or no Community, the reality is that most of us have no experience building one. Third Places were always part of the fabric of our parents' and grandparents' lives, practically invisible, passed on from generation to generation, and no one ever taught us how to cultivate our own. This is a large part of why I am writing this book. I believe that what is needed most in the world right now is the power of Community, our Third Place.

Current State...

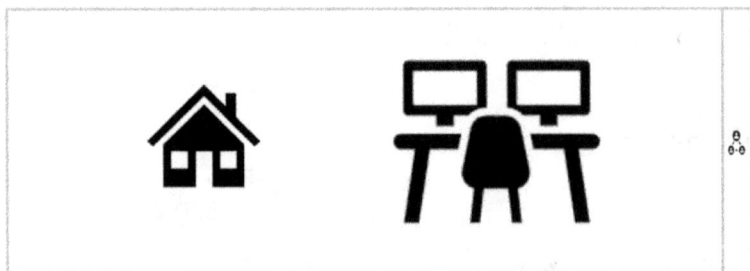

The reason I am standing here today is because of the power of my Third Place, my Community. That is why I'm so passionate about the work we've been doing at EDGE Leadership the last twelve years, building Third Places inside companies through curating peer mentoring and group coaching circles. For people to develop fruitful Third Places, we must meet them where they spend the majority of their time. For the vast majority, that is at work.

There is a real value for companies to support Third Places. First, from an integrity standpoint, whether we realize it or not, our organizations have blurred boundaries between our personal and professional lives in ways that we need to acknowledge and take ownership for. Second, because the research is crystal clear, happy people who are living a fulfilled life are better workers. They are more engaged, more productive, and more innovative. Because people today often lack the physical Third Places of the past, we need to be creative and search out, join, or, if needed, create our own.

DEVELOPING OUR PERSONAL AND PROFESSIONAL COMMUNITIES

Since 2013, we have tested and refined the PEER Technology Framework in Fortune 500 companies with people at every level of the Professional Growth Mountain. We've helped create Third Spaces focused on sharing best practices as peers in the Early Career Field, in the Mid-Career Woods, and also in the rocky, craggy area of managing directors, officers, and VPs, which I often refer to as the Summit.

In fact, as of this writing, our team of coaches at EDGE Leadership has engaged more than 12,000 leaders globally in the last twelve years through PEER mentoring and group Coaching Circles, not only for high-potential leaders but across the landscape of companies, driving culture change and improved mental health and well-being for people at all levels of their career.

As a pioneer in the space of peer learning and group coaching, I've found that the Growth Mountain and Wayfinding Compass concept helps connect dots across a map that most of us didn't even know was there, making the invisible visible. When combined with the PEER Technology Framework, it's what companies don't even know they need because until now, there simply hasn't been a consistent way to leverage personal *and* professional knowledge transfer across an organization.

For example, inside a mid-career peer group coaching cohort for a large multinational firm, everyone may be in the woods together, but likely they're all on different sides of the mountain. So we can gain great value when we discuss best practices and lessons learned with one another.

I'd recommend not touching the berry bushes on the southern-facing ridge because they made me sick for days. But there is an empty cave at the foot of the waterfall on the northern side, and it is a great shelter during a storm.

This horizontal knowledge transfer between mid-career folks across the mountain is a game-changer. Imagine if I had it when I first became a people manager at Bayer and failed miserably. Maybe I could have had a chance to succeed because I would have had access to so much more relevant and timely information to Wayfind my course with intention.

And yet the power of horizontal knowledge transfer peer-to-peer has an inherent limitation: *We don't know what we don't know.* And that is why we also need vertical knowledge transfer that engages folks *between* mountain levels.

For example, on the Entrepreneur Growth Mountain—one I have trekked twice since EDGE Leadership is my second coaching company—while some may be in the Starting-a-Company Field, others are higher up in the Scaling-the-Business Woods and can offer some guidance for trekking up to that next level.

Or perhaps on a Personal Growth Mountain in the case of families like mine with a child who transitioned genders, many of us in the Shock and Awe Field are desperately looking up at those in the Settling-into-Our-New-Reality Woods for some encouragement.

Whichever Growth Mountain or phase you're on, the good news is that the Wayfinding process is exactly the same, whether it's business or personal.

As we evolve in our careers and lives, we naturally want to discover where people in our circle are on their own mountain treks. We also want to understand what developmental spaces we are in so we can begin to foster connections that will ultimately help all of us navigate our own journeys or explorations more effectively.

Some folks may be content with their relationships on their current Professional Growth Mountain inside their company but want to increase their credibility and visibility in their industry or field in the coming year. Perhaps they want to represent their organization at a conference or sit on a panel and share their expertise, thus building their *external strategic network.*

In this case, their desired mountain trek for that year would be outside of their organization and focused on building credibility *inside their industry.* Other people may be focused on their strategic network inside their company, trying to position themselves for a promotion.

For still others, their Wayfinding path this year may be on a Community Growth Mountain, building their Third Place for themselves and their families. Perhaps their goal is to expand their impact in their city, so they chart a course to sit on a nonprofit board. To do that well, they will need to build an intentional strategic network in their local region, likely across companies and industries.

And of course, there is always the Personal Growth Mountain everyone must navigate where the weather is always shifting around marriage, parenthood, health, well-being, personal evolution, extended family, and friendships. Some may even choose to relocate, navigating away from the mountains they know well to instead explore new lands.

⊕ FIELD NOTES

In my experience coaching over the last three decades, people often have the most success when they can truly focus on one Growth Mountain at a time. Whatever area on whichever mountain you currently find yourself— or wherever you aspire to grow next—the Wayfinding questions are the same.

- Do you want to climb higher, or are you content for now where you are? Why?

- Where are you feeling inadequate? What technical or soft skill gaps do you have?

- What do you want in order to move forward?

- To achieve that, can you stay on this mountain, or is it time to Wayfind a new path and explore another?

As you may recall, when I was a salesperson in the Early Career Fields of healthcare at Johnson & Johnson, I was airlifted (quite unsuccessfully) into the deep Mid-Career Woods with little to no rations, zero survival skills, and no experience Wayfinding on my own. Thanks to the potential Bayer saw in me, I trekked back to the base of a new Professional Growth Mountain (Human Resources) and started my journey in the Early Career Field of Learning and Development.

Over the next ten years, I scaled up into the Mid-Career Woods with plenty of real-life experience and now, thankfully, with a strategic network to support me. Later, I Wayfound up to the rocky, craggy Summit in my field when I was promoted to Director of Organization Development and eventually to Vice President of Human Resources in the construction industry. And yet as my personal evolution continued and after living on the Summit for a few years, I decided to change course yet again and dropped down to the Early Career Fields at the base of a new Mountain Range of Entrepreneurship. I began my Wayfinding all over again.

Many of us will reinvent ourselves four, five, or even six (or more) times across our career, starting each time at the base of a different Professional Growth Mountain. The analyst living in a treehouse in the Mid-Career Woods of a Fortune 500 Company Mountain becomes a brand-new nurse at the base of a larger Mountain farther north. The VP of Sales who used to sit and strategize on the rocky cliffs of the Summit at sunset becomes an entrepreneur, deep in the Early Career weeds, and spends their days executing results as a consultant and a new vendor to the company they once led.

On the Personal Growth Mountain front, a single person gets married or a middle-aged person finds themselves suddenly divorced and back in the Dating Field for the first time in seventeen years at the base of an entirely new Personal Growth Mountain.

In my case, I have climbed five distinct Professional Growth Mountains across my career, and I am not even fifty years old. As you know, my first career was in sales. Then I was a leadership coach who became an HR executive who became an entrepreneur, a corporate board director, and then reinvented myself as a speaker and an author.

As of this writing, after publishing three books and becoming a global keynote, I evolved in 2023 yet again, shifting from my expertise in the leadership space to bravely stepping into the Early Career Fields to study mental well-being, energy management, and resilience. I began my trek to become a Reiki Master and expert in the space of personal evolution in a professional setting.

For each of us, understanding where we are on our current Growth Mountain and then identifying who is around us, above us, and below us is like transforming an old-school compass and map and converting them to a 3D GPS app powered by generative AI, complete with traffic notifications and just-in-time rerouting.

The points of Self-Awareness, Self-Alignment, Self-Trust, and Self-Worth on our Wayfinding Compass provide powerful personal strategic planning and are fueled by the peers in our Third Place. Together they guide us as we chart our chosen career and life paths and enable us to understand what, when, and how to leverage them as resources while simultaneously providing the constant opportunity to *be* those resources to others because we were never meant to travel alone.

THE TOPOGRAPHY OF THE MOUNTAIN RANGES IN OUR LIVES

When it came time for me to be life-flighted out of the Mid-Career Woods in Sales Management at Bayer, I thankfully landed at the base of a completely different mountain range of HR, Coaching, and Organization Development. Once I got acclimated to the atmosphere there, I ultimately took a different path that led to yet another Growth Mountain range. That was when I started my own business and became a solopreneur of my first company, Red Zebra Consulting, at the age of twenty-seven.

To give you a feel for my experience, it was like going from a tropical jungle mountain in South America to the Swiss Alps. It was a whole different career path with a whole new set of challenges. As I read other people's books about starting a business, it was almost like I was reading the maps other explorers had left behind. Again, my sales experience came in handy as I marketed myself and my new business to both Bayer and Johnson & Johnson, places where I already had built strong relationships and trust. My goal was to help them develop their Millennial talent so future leaders would be better prepared than I had been.

Ultimately, I spent three years as the founder of Red Zebra, focusing solely on coaching early-career Millennials. But I struggled with my Wayfinding as a new solopreneur, and I soon figured out why. I had two big strikes against me.

The first was that I was a twenty-seven-year-old leadership coach and consultant competing with coaches thirty years my senior. The second was that I was ahead of the market. Very few folks in leadership noticed any pain points specific to the

Millennial generation. At the time, while companies would invest in coaching for executives, they certainly weren't budgeting in 2004 for coaching early or mid-career talent. And even the definition of coaching was limited to one-on-one coaching in most companies. Group coaching, my personal passion, was still in its infancy.

As I came to realize, companies needed more time to know that lecture-based, slideshow training classes are less effective with my fellow Millennials than previous generations. The world wasn't quite ready for the innovation of peer mentoring and group coaching that I wanted to bring to traditional training and development programs.

And that's the thing about mountains, isn't it? We can have everything we need all packed neatly in our sleek, nylon backpacks alongside our best innovative techniques. And if the weather isn't amenable to climbing or the world isn't ready for your ideas, you just have to wait. Much like a snowstorm that will keep you holed up where you are, you have to be patient until the elements clear and you can see your path to Wayfind to the next level.

When I realized my path wasn't clear yet and might not be for the foreseeable future, I knew I needed to pivot. In 2007, I was hired by one of my clients, a regional general contractor, to support the transition of the company from a father to his sons, the oldest of whom was forty. I was tasked with supporting the new all-Millennial leadership team and building a robust people-first culture. And that is how I became one of the first in-house coaches in the construction industry.

While I still found myself on the Professional Growth Mountain of Coaching, which I had become accustomed to, it was certainly a very different face of the mountain. In-house coaching is a whole other terrain compared to being an external coach.

While navigating this change, I also ascended from the Mid-Career Woods to my first mountain Summit two years later when I was named the company's first female Vice President.

This was a huge step, not only for me navigating a new area of my Professional Growth Mountain but also for the organization in general. Never before in their twenty-eight-year history had they had a woman in the role of people manager, let alone on the executive team. To say there were no tracks for me to follow in my Wayfinding efforts would be a vast understatement.

While I was making this progress on my Professional Mountain, I simultaneously found myself Wayfinding a different journey on my Personal Growth Mountain. I was thrilled to be skyrocketing up my professional path but was struggling deeply to navigate my personal one. I found myself approaching my second marriage with trepidation and fear. I was first married at the age of twenty-one, and I carried the unfortunate baggage, as many of us do, of not wanting to mess up this new relationship, especially with my son Eli joining me on the adventure.

I felt extremely lonely on my Personal Growth Mountain journey and, although I didn't have the language for it at the time, in desperate need of a Third Place. I was ambitious and driven to pursue my career coaching passion in my Second Place: Work. And I was struggling to balance what felt like competing Growth Mountains. How could I have a successful career and also balance what felt like the competing demands of my First Place: Home? I wanted desperately to be a good wife to my new husband, Kevin, while also being the best possible mom to Eli.

As I looked at my personal relationships with friends, I also didn't see any choosing to follow my same path. Many opted to become stay-at-home moms or scale back their careers to part-time, a choice I respected deeply but knew wasn't in my plans. Having navigated a divorce in my twenties, I knew I would always prioritize my financial independence, and for me, that meant working full-time. Period.

It was about this time that my mother reminded me that as humans we aren't meant to scale our mountains alone. We were meant to live in villages, tribes, and communities. While she didn't use the term Third Places, of course, I remember her saying to me, "Have you ever heard of someone climbing Everest by themself? Or migrating across America on the Oregon Trail alone? No. And for good reason."

The unhealthy obsession here in America on extreme self-reliance is antiquated and self-destructive. We are only doing a disservice to ourselves and our overall well-being by attempting to survive, much less to thrive on our own.

I knew in my Belly that I needed to find a group of people who were in that same developmental space, navigating their own Growth Mountains across their First and Second Places so we could help one another. Urged by my mother to find a peer group to support my Wayfinding efforts in my personal life, I founded a community of working mothers in my hometown that not only saved me from this terrifying solo climb but also inspired the innovations that would become my life's work. I had no idea what I needed at that time in my life, but it was easy to see I couldn't do it alone.

In the midst of that steep, uphill climb in my career as I was desperately Wayfinding my journey as one of the first in-house coaches in the construction industry, and with storms of change and uncertainty blowing across my Personal Growth Mountain, the one thing I knew for sure was that I needed to find someone who had *been there, done that.* And I also knew that I wanted support both from a leadership *and* a life standpoint. I not only wanted to connect with a mentor who knew how to navigate the challenge I was facing as the first woman VP in the male-dominated industry of construction but who could also appreciate all I was trying to navigate as a new wife and mother.

I started looking around the Pittsburgh region. The first thing I learned seems rather obvious now. You can't ask a stranger to be your mentor. The answer is almost always going to be no, or at least it was in my case.

So I did the next best thing. I started going anywhere professional women met, hopping from networking group to networking group all over the city. Although those meetings were mostly enjoyable, the experience often felt inauthentic and superficial. What I was really craving was a genuine connection and development within a peer group that would support my Wayfinding and help me feel less alone on my journey of personal evolution. I needed a Third Place that brought both vulnerability and consistency.

Seeking genuine connection has always been so purposeful for me because I believe in the awesome power of human potential. Everyone boldly starts in their trek up their Growth Mountain as if they're on a path of personal achievement. We try, we fail, we overcome. We learn, work hard, and receive accolades for a job well done *as individuals.*

We each tend to view the world as if we're in the spotlight alone, especially in the Early Career Fields with all the attention and responsibility resting on one set of shoulders—our own. And yet as we grow and evolve in our lives, somehow achieving great results simply isn't enough anymore. It doesn't serve us on our journey the way it once did. We begin to feel stuck.

Even our own Self-Awareness is limited when it is solely navel-gazing. As humans, we were never meant to survive much less thrive on our own. We need the support of our peers coming alongside us and joining us in our Wayfinding journeys.

It is at this crucial pivotal point where the focus must shift from seeking personal achievements to searching for ways to contribute to others. It's the difference between one lantern barely lighting the way on a path through the forest and the collective lights of many illuminating a broader way, making navigation infinitely much easier.

I began to learn this truth quite by accident. As I went from one women's networking event to the next, I started finding amazing women, my peers across companies and industries from whom I wanted to learn.

In fact, the man who would later become my husband, Kevin, told me during that time that it was as if I were collecting women like jewels on a crown. I had begun to find relationships and authentic connections, but I had not yet discovered the Third Place I needed to navigate my Growth Mountains with confidence.

What I wanted was personal evolution alongside other women, a brave and vulnerable space to learn what was working for them, what wasn't working so well and why, and how to apply those best practices and lessons learned in my Wayfinding. As a Millennial, I also knew I needed an intentional learning framework with those critical relationships built into it.

When I couldn't find the peer-to-peer mentoring circle I wanted, I realized I would need to create it. Fortunately for me, the experiences I had from my time at Red Zebra Consulting proved the exact compass I needed to chart my course.

Self-discovery is rarely successful on your own. Even the best app or self-paced developmental activity in the world is no replacement for sharing a journey beside someone and having peer accountability. I discovered that I could have all the Self-Awareness in the world, but if I didn't walk in alignment with what really mattered to me, my personal evolution was limited.

And the pressure, I felt, was *on*.

After all, if I was going to be big and bold, the first female VP my company had ever seen, what responsibility did I have to every other woman in that organization? Even though I was only thirty-two years old, the other women across the company would be looking to me. But I had no clue how to inspire and bring value to them. And I didn't believe I was good enough. Who was *I* to mentor *them*? My Inner Critic and self-limiting belief systems were obviously working overtime.

The very first PEER mentoring cohort I created in 2007, that I would now refer to as a Third Place, was a small group of working mothers just like me. At the time, that was where I personally felt I needed the most support, just like my mother had advised me. We got together on a monthly basis and followed a simple Peer Mentoring Mastermind format.

As we journeyed together across a decade, we formed a steadfast group of mutual support, much like the interconnected points on a compass rose. We deepened each other's Self-Awareness by forming the foundation of our Self-Alignment. As a coach, I know full well that adults do not change behaviors on their own. Rare is the person who has the discipline to do that. So the best practice is to enroll accountability partners, peers who will provide feedback and perspective, who will follow up with us about the things that matter most, and who will ensure that we walk in alignment with our core values, purpose, and goals.

In our cohort, we celebrated each other's triumphs, offered unwavering support during testing times at work and at home, and provided a space where each member could hone their ability to seek guidance and assistance. The age-old saying "Two heads are better than one" captures the essence of our Peer Mentoring experience. Just as a compass derives its strength from multiple cardinal points working in harmony, our collective thinking generated outcomes that surpassed the capabilities of any individual thought or idea.

Together as peers we challenged one another to dive into Self-Awareness and figure out our own Wantings in our First and Second Places. We built Self-Trust by honoring what mattered most to each of us, sharing best practices and lessons learned as we each endeavored to walk in Self-Alignment. And many of us, myself included, found a real sense of Self-Worth as well.

When our individual and unique perspectives work in harmony with others, we get collective engagement, empowerment, and change. We learn that everyone, especially those we may not have expected, has something to contribute because each voice carries with it a lifetime of experience, education, wisdom, and insights. When we change as individuals, we change as a collective.

The more I began showing up for myself, thanks to the accountability provided by my peers, I started to prioritize my own wants and needs almost as much as I prioritized others. For the first time in my life, I began treating myself as I would my very best friend. This Self-Trust is built brick by brick, slowly, and over time on our Wayfinding journey when we prove to ourselves that we are dependable. And from there, Self-Trust forms the foundation of Self-Worth, or what I like to call self-love.

WAYFINDING THROUGH PEER DEVELOPMENT

What was unique about the initial working mothers' group that we named EMPOWER was that we had mothers from all across the spectrum. This Third Place brought together mothers across the parenting stages with children in kindergarten (like mine), middle school, high school, and even college. We had married moms and single moms, straight moms and gay moms, new moms and seasoned ones. It was amazingly powerful, although at the time, it was invisible to me that this first peer mentoring experience included women from different places and spaces in life.

As a result of this rich diversity (a hallmark of a powerful Third Place, by the way), we all benefited from both vertical and horizontal knowledge transfer taking place at the same time, offering insights from everyone's treks across their own Personal and Professional Growth Mountains and enhancing the creation of each other's Wayfinding Compass.

When I as the mother of a kindergartner bemoaned what was happening in my life and then felt guilty about struggling, trapped by my own limiting belief system, a more seasoned mother stepped up to share insight, perspective, and feedback, challenging my Self-Awareness and Self-Alignment. I remember one woman saying to me, "I hear you. I've been there. But in my experience, what you're worrying about may not be important in the grand scheme of things. And I think what you said earlier about what happened on the playground last week may be more critical to explore. Here's why."

That level of honest, experienced insight—Peer Mentoring at its best—might not have happened if we hadn't had a brave Third Place to be vulnerable with such a diverse group of women. This was the power of a peer group to amplify both Self-Awareness (what I think I know about myself, which shifts as I evolve) and Self-Alignment (focus on what matters) in action.

After two years, the success of that first informal peer group spawned a high-potential professional women's group in the Pittsburgh region that we playfully named the Circle of Trust (CoT) after the movie *Meet the Parents* that had been a big hit a few years before. Now, in addition to hosting EMPOWER at my kitchen table each month, I met with this group of young women to create another Third Place for myself.

This group represented women across companies and industries, and we met consistently on a monthly basis, rotating from kitchen table to kitchen table across the region. We vulnerably shared best practices and lessons learned both at work and at home, once again supporting one another in our Wayfinding journeys across our Growth Mountains and through our individual personal evolution.

And yet because we were truly peers, all in our late twenties to early thirties and with similar career experiences, trying to navigate the transition from Early Career Fields to Mid-Career Woods, we quickly found out that peer learning has an inherent limitation. *We didn't know what we didn't know.* As the group's unofficial facilitator, I could see that if we were going to progress to this new frontier, we had to give ourselves permission to become even more vulnerable and ask for help outside the cohort.

As I reflected on what made the EMPOWER working mothers' group so successful, I recognized the value of vertical knowledge transfer clearly for the first time. I realized that as a group of early career leaders fresh in our marriages (some of us with littles at home) in the Early Career Fields, we needed to add people with more experience in order for us to achieve our personal evolution goals. And so, by leveraging the power of our collective networks, the new CoT cohort members acted as compass points, guiding us toward more seasoned Mid-Career leaders farther up the Growth Mountain to willingly share their knowledge and experience with us.

Together we chose the personal and professional topics we were stuck on each year and invited these guides from the Mid-Career Woods to join us in our Third Place as guest mentors. They met our vulnerability with their own by engaging in an authentic dialogue with us and sharing their lessons learned from their respective mountain treks. Our little CoT cohort blossomed and started to get visibility with more and more leaders from both corporate and nonprofit organizations across industries. Soon we had a waiting list of executives around Pittsburgh who wanted to engage with this professional development cohort of young women.

About eighteen months later, a national mentoring organization called Strong Women, Strong Girls (SWSG) asked if I would be interested in building a leadership development experience pro bono for them based on what I had learned in my group coaching experiences. An executive on their board of directors had served as a guest mentor to the CoT and suggested a partnership. SWSG wanted to get more young Millennial women to volunteer with the organization, and their hope was that companies would sponsor high-potential women to go through their development program in a way that would create sustainable corporate giving for their nonprofit.

After launching a cohort of women in Pittsburgh in 2010, SWSG asked me to expand my volunteer work, sit on their national board of directors, and help them launch another high-potential women's cohort in Boston—and another in Miami. Keep in mind that I still had my full-time job as the Vice President of Human Resources. But I also knew this supportive process of personal evolution, building these Third Places, was fueling my soul in a way my job really wasn't anymore. I could see this peer-centered, group-coaching dynamic was both unique and powerful. And I knew in my heart that I had to figure out how to bring it into more people's lives. While my day job as the head of HR certainly challenged my brain, I realized this group coaching work was igniting me in a way I never could have imagined, and I knew it was time to move Growth Mountains again.

We can only successfully Wayfind and build Third Places through sustaining authentic relationships with one another as peers. Wayfinding is essentially a human task, finding our way home to ourselves again. And as I hope you know by now, personal evolution—despite its name—is not a solitary act. It is communal. As we evolve, as we heal, we unconsciously give others permission to do the same. Our peers, like our core values, aligned behaviors, types of rest, new belief systems, and energy regulation skills picked up along the Wayfinding journey, are all as critical to our progress as they are to our health and well-being.

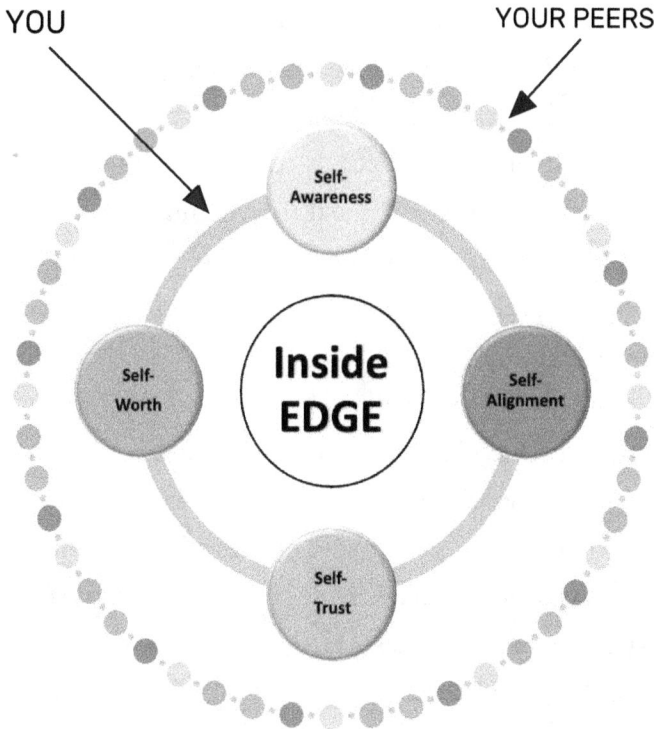

YOU YOUR PEERS

Self-Awareness

Self-Worth

Inside EDGE

Self-Alignment

Self-Trust

What I have learned from my personal evolution and has been reinforced by building hundreds of Third Places is this: I am only a "self" in relation to others. Self-Awareness is forever limited if we're alone with our thoughts and a journal, book, app or podcast. Only when we introduce a Third Place can our peers serve as a mirror to not only reflect feedback, perspectives, and insights but also challenge our self-limiting belief systems, cultural conditioning, and other things that do not serve us. The spirit of self needs other humans to witness it. It desires a deep, attuned presence to flourish when we can embrace curiosity and see ourselves and our greatness through the eyes of other humans who care about us.

In my nearly three decades as an executive and leadership coach while Wayfinding through the often treacherous terrains of both Personal and Professional Growth Mountains, I've discovered the essential role of Mentors, Coaches, and Advocates, each supporting the Personal Evolution dial points on our Wayfinding Compass. The relationship with each of the three Mountain Guides is always set against the backdrop of the relationship that we have with ourselves. Each relationship is always seen and maximized in the relationship through us.

In order to maximize the Mountain Guides we seek out, we must first have clarity for our Wayfinding Compass. Self-Awareness is understanding who you truly are, what drives you, what you truly want, and where you excel. Self-Alignment is aligning your actions, values, and goals with intentional rest and recovery cycles so you harness the energy needed to move forward with confidence and clarity. Self-Trust is building the courage to trust your instincts, befriend your Inner Critic, set and sustain boundaries to make bold decisions that matter, and take risks. Self-Worth is recognizing the value you bring to the table and how that impacts your self-view as much as it does your family, friends, teams, and organizations, and intentionally reprogramming your belief systems.

Now that we have calibrated our Wayfinding Compass, we have a connection with ourselves, our goals, our desires, and our dreams. No matter how the terrain shifts, no matter what storm blows over the horizon, when we have clarity about who we are and don't feel alone, we can successfully navigate whatever life brings us. And we're ready to find the Mountain Guides who will accompany us successfully on our journey. The power that Mountain Guides bring us is new perspective and wise experience, but in order to benefit from them, we have to lean into vulnerability and practice the skill of receiving. We have to ask for help.

8

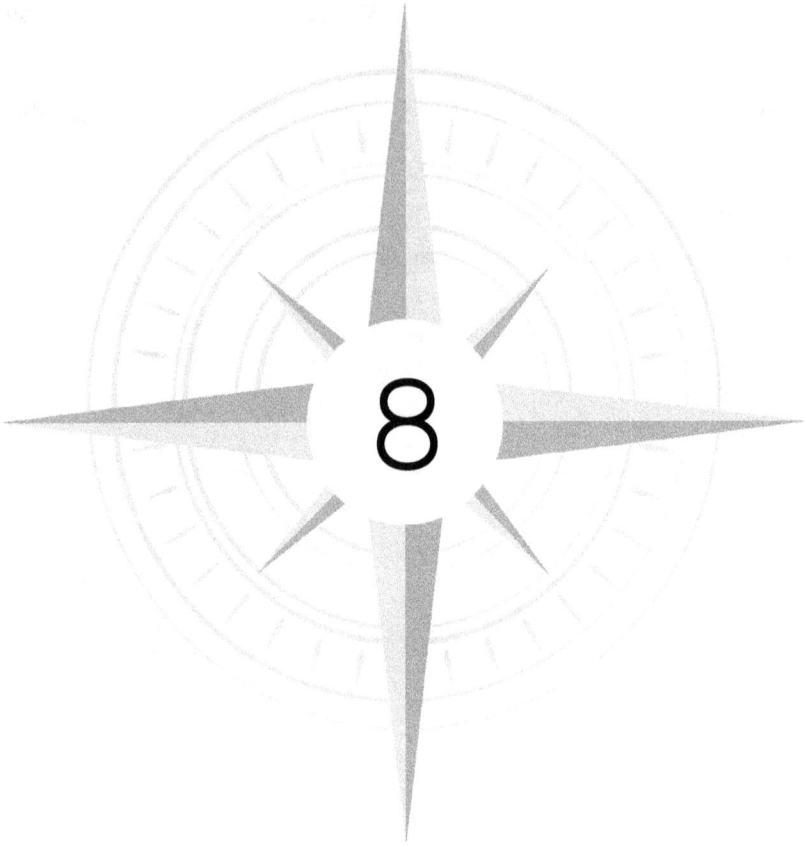

YOUR COMPANIONS
The Three Wayfinding
Mountain Guides

Just as life's weather and conditions can change on the different mountain faces, unexpected challenges may disrupt your Wayfinding efforts. It's during those times you encounter unforeseen obstacles that you find yourself in uncharted territory. This is why it is crucial to cultivate a strategic network that supports your Wayfinding Compass throughout your Personal and Professional Growth Mountain journeys. When you glance at your trusted Mountain

Guides and realize that none of them have experience on this particular Mountain, it becomes evident that it's time to expand your network and seek those who can provide the guidance you need.

Meeting with a community of peers, building a Third Place together, and learning about the environment on your Growth Mountain can be the difference between Wayfinding success and struggle. If you are strategic in your personal evolution journey through Self-Awareness to Self-Alignment, and from Self-Trust to Self-Worth, you will understand when and where you need new Mountain Guides. I consider this process something like nature's way of shedding or pruning to allow for new growth. Without this process, we delay or stunt in ourselves all the amazing possibilities that lie ahead.

As you move to different terrains or faces of your Personal and Professional Growth Mountains like I did so many times, you will naturally find new Mountain Guides along the way. Other times, you will need to be intentional about seeking them out. This may come in the form of networking opportunities, both new and old, virtual and in person. While you may not need a particular Mountain Guide at that specific time, you may ultimately have a need for one where you are headed.

Herminia Ibarra, a leading expert on professional networks, identifies several types of networks that can be instrumental on our journey: Operational Networks, Personal Networks, and Strategic Networks.[12] Operational Networks often include the people you work with daily. Personal Networks are typically friends and family. And Strategic Networks comprise individuals who can open doors to new opportunities. And when done well, most strategic networks can also become Third Places.

In the context of our Wayfinding journey, think of Operational Networks as the team of Mountain Guides you rely on for the day-to-day challenges and navigating the familiar terrains of your current Growth Mountain. Personal Networks, on the other hand, provide the emotional support and encouragement to keep you going when the path gets tough. These networks serve as your companions and fellow Wayfinders.

Strategic Networks are like experienced guides who can lead you to uncharted territories and connect you with other experts. Advocates share opportunity, Mentors share knowledge, and Coaches empower the discipline and resilience needed to go the distance. Together, these three critical roles hold all the keys to scale new peaks and pathways across our Growth Mountains.

Sometimes you may not know you need a Strategic Network until you encounter unfamiliar terrain or a daunting obstacle. At such times, actively expanding your Strategic Network can be what you need to guide you through the uncertainty and help you navigate unexplored territories.

In your professional life, that may mean joining professional networks or, if you can find them, Third Places in your area of expertise, gender, profession, or age group. For example, you could join a Young Professional Group when you are just starting out or something more niche like a Women Accounting Professionals Network. For my Wayfinding journey, a great example of this was most certainly the Circle of Trust.

In your personal life, finding Third Places is much the same. Some of us have found powerful connections through social media channels. Whether it's a mothers' group or an LGBTQ+ entrepreneur network, there are online peer groups of every kind for every age, situation, and topic. These connectors provide understanding, knowledge, and experience in the things you may be facing, just like EMPOWER, the working moms' group that shifted my whole career trajectory.

⊕ **FIELD NOTES**

Remember that the criteria for what makes a powerful Third Place are two things: vulnerability and consistency. As you search, I invite you to ask yourself questions such as "How often does the group meet?" "What kind of container exists that allows for trust to build?" "Can I show up as my whole self, personally and professionally?"

Navigating the diverse landscapes of Growth Mountains demands a strategic and evolving network to match the changing conditions and terrains you encounter.[13] Ibarra's research underscores the importance of not only having the right Mountain Guides but also continually reassessing your network, which is why our Wayfinding Compass is only complete with the knowledge that we can also rely on our own inner wisdom to guide us along our Wayfinding journey.

Much like a compass guiding explorers through unfamiliar territories, your network should adapt to the evolving challenges and uncharted peaks of your journey. As you ascend your Growth Mountains, I invite you to consider the composition of your own current strategic network or Third Place and whether it aligns with your immediate Wayfinding needs.

Are there new Mountain Guides to recruit? Are there uncharted paths to explore? Just as seasoned Wayfinders update their maps to reflect the changing terrain, we too must assess and adjust our network to ensure we have the support and guidance required for each leg of our journey.

Recognizing that our trusted Mountain Guides may change over time, both in purpose and proximity, is a vital aspect of this journey and why being in peer mentoring and coaching circles can be a powerful addition. Embracing the natural process of shedding old connections allows for the growth of new possibilities. Whether you organically discover new Mountain Guides on your path or actively seek them out through intentional networking efforts, the value of diverse peer connections while Wayfinding through your personal evolution cannot be overstated.

In both professional and personal spheres, joining (or in my case, building) Third Places to learn and grow beside your peers provides a reservoir of understanding, knowledge, and shared experiences. But as I said earlier, peer learning has an inherent limitation. We don't know what we don't know. And that is where our Mountain Guides come in, serving as Mentors, Coaches, and Advocates. And I will tell you most earnestly that these three roles have served as indispensable guides to me through the intricate trails of my life's Growth Mountains.

OUR THREE MOUNTAIN GUIDES: MENTOR, COACH, AND ADVOCATE

We begin by focusing on our Mentor Mountain Guide. Like the sun rising in the East, mentorship is something almost all of us inherently recognize as essential to navigating our personal and professional Growth Mountains. Mentoring, by definition, is an unequal power relationship between two individuals—one an expert with significant experience and the other a learner, ready to absorb new knowledge. Mentors aren't necessarily older; for instance, one of my current Mentors is twenty-three years old.

A Mentor Mountain Guide is someone who simply has more domain experience and Wayfinding knowledge on a particular Growth Mountain. This relationship is defined by the Mentor's role to share their knowledge with their mentee. As Mentors share stories, experiences, and best practices, mentees gain insights from someone who has navigated the path before. Mentors often provide advice, feedback, or even direct suggestions based on their experiences.

However, mentoring can sometimes miss the mark. For instance, a woman of color in her late twenties may struggle to relate to a much older white male Mentor's advice. In navigating my Growth Mountains, I sometimes followed my Mentor's guidance and sometimes didn't, based on my own Wayfinding Compass. While sometimes their stories can offer incredible insight and value, sometimes their advice may be outdated or irrelevant, like when they are cautioning about bears by the old cave next to the waterfall, deep in the Mid-Career Woods, that you know full well no longer live there.

This is where our second Mountain Guide, a Coach, can offer a fresh and needed perspective in our Wayfinding journey. Coaches provide a different type of guidance, focusing on helping us find our own path rather than relying solely on sharing their past experiences.

Unlike mentoring, coaching is an equal power relationship. Coaches don't tell you what to do; they ask thoughtful questions that empower you to find your own solutions. For this reason, our Coach Mountain Guide lives in the West where the sun sets and the moon rises.

As a Coach for nearly three decades, I've come to love how coaching creates the capacity for individuals to think critically through their own issues. Coaches don't give advice or expect to have the answers like Mentors do. Instead, they offer support, accountability, and companionship as people chart their course and explore possibilities. Coaches are critical to our Wayfinding Compass, helping us find our own True North.

The truth is that the best solutions to our struggles usually come from within. No one understands a challenge like the person facing it. However, finding the space to actively work through challenges can be difficult, as illustrated in my opening story.

As a salesperson at Johnson & Johnson, I realized I wanted to become a sales manager. After deciding to make that move, I left the Early Career Fields of Johnson & Johnson for a completely different mountain with Bayer at the Mid-Career Woods. Though still in the healthcare industry, everything was different—the weather, terrain, vegetation, food sources, and predators. And as you know full well at this point, I had no idea where to start.

Change is inevitable in both your personal and professional life. We get laid off, start new jobs, get married, have a baby, or lose a parent. Transition is the psychological process of moving through change, and in my own Wayfinding journey, healthy transitions are best navigated with a Coach by our side.

Through each transition (read: reinvention) in my career and life, I've realized that we always start at the bottom of a new Growth Mountain. After leaving Bayer to start my first coaching company, Red Zebra, at the base of the Entrepreneurship Mountain, I realized I not only needed new gear but also new knowledge. That meant going back to school, getting my professional coaching certification, gaining experience as an external Coach, and of course, hiring a Coach to support me through it all.

While our first two Mountain Guides, the Mentor and the Coach, play crucial roles in guiding us through the challenges and uncertainties of our Growth Mountains, we cannot rely solely on them. The Mentor shares pivotal knowledge, and the Coach helps manage our mindset, but we also need a third Mountain Guide—an Advocate.

Advocates bring influence and expertise born from firsthand experience, introducing us to new opportunities and uncharted territories. The Advocate Mountain Guide, offering a unique perspective to Wayfinding, ensures a well-rounded expedition across our Growth Mountains.

Advocate Mountain Guides, like Mentor Mountain Guides, also have an unequal power relationship. While Mentors transfer knowledge, Advocates provide opportunities. Advocates are essential for bringing up our names in the rooms that we are not in. They connect us to opportunities and help us advance on our Personal and Professional Growth Mountains.

Advocates speak on our behalf in rooms where we are not present, and in doing so, they can powerfully link talent, life, career, and results. When I coach high-potential managers in the Mid-Career Woods of large organizations, I advise them that their best Advocate is likely someone two levels above them who has visibility over the broader terrain. This higher-level visibility of the Summit allows Advocates to see above the treetops and identify opportunities and dangers such as a coming avalanche we can't see from deep within the forest.

All our Mountain Guides share a common goal: they genuinely care about us and our goals and want to see us succeed. Mentors and Coaches give back because someone once did the same for them, and it feels good to help others. Mentoring others also makes us feel competent and confident, adding value to the relationship. Yet Advocate Mountain Guides are different from

Mentors, and this is an important distinction to note. There is an unspoken quid pro quo in advocacy relationships. Advocates look for two specific things.

> **Excellence in Results:** If we don't deliver excellent results, our Advocates won't continue to advocate for us. Lending their name and credibility to us means expecting our top performance.

> **Valuable Feedback and Insight:** Advocates seek feedback and insights to achieve their strategic goals. For example, someone in the Mid-Career Woods can provide perspectives that a leader near the mountaintop cannot see. Perhaps your Advocate is planning a new strategy and believes we can't go to the western face of the mountain because of the bear clan that lives by the waterfall. Your insight may be that the bears moved out about five years ago, and now that cave is a mighty great place to wait out a storm. Sharing relevant insights about what's happening deep in the Mid-Career Woods or even down in the Early-Career Fields helps our Advocates shape stronger strategies.

If these expectations aren't met—delivering excellent results and offering meaningful insights—the advocacy relationship fades. The Advocate relationship should be honored as an equal exchange of delivering results and sharing insights, forming a foundation for enduring partnerships.

MY ADVOCATE MOUNTAIN GUIDE: DIRECTING OPPORTUNITIES

When I was in my early thirties, I wanted to focus on my Community Growth Mountain. I had settled into my role as Vice President of Human Resources and was feeling confident in my internal corporate Professional Growth Mountain. We were winning regional and national awards for our Leadership and Development programming. I was excited to be representing my company on the national stage, my external industry Professional Growth Mountain, and was intentionally building my external network in powerful ways too.

My Personal Growth Mountain finally felt settled (thank goodness), and I knew it was time to think about how I could bring value to the region of Pittsburgh and my community. After building the pro bono group coaching programs with Strong Women, Strong Girls across the country, I knew I wanted to sit on a nonprofit board to enhance my leadership capability, but I also knew that wasn't going to just happen. I needed to activate and leverage my strategic network.

After I shared my interest with some local executives, including a few guest mentors from the Circle of Trust, I received the offer to serve on a committee for a large nonprofit called the Allegheny Conference, Pittsburgh's public/private partnership focused on improving the economic future of the city. It was there that I met Laura Ellsworth. Laura was a Partner-in-Charge of an influential law firm, Jones Day, and is a total powerhouse in my local community of Pittsburgh still to this day, fifteen years later.

I admit I had a bit of a girl crush on Laura from afar, but

I was incredibly grateful for the opportunity and visibility she offered me at the Allegheny Conference. I put my head down and went to work, bringing value to the committee any way I could. Within six months, more opportunities started coming my way such as speaking at a large regional event, serving on two more committees, and finally, after one year, being invited to sit on my first nonprofit board.

It was about then that I started getting curious about how these opportunities were finding me. As it turned out, they all came through someone who, unbeknownst to me, had been advocating for me—Laura Ellsworth. She had been acting as my Advocate Mountain Guide all along.

As a student of leadership development, I knew if I wanted these opportunities to continue to flow my way, I needed to start bringing consistent value to Laura in the form of feedback and perspective. When I thought about where Laura was on my local Community Growth Mountain, I understood she was right near the Summit while I was brand new to the Early Career Fields of nonprofit service at the base of this mountain.

At her level, Laura's role was to look into the future of the Pittsburgh region and beyond, across the miles of plains in the distance, and think big and strategically. As I continued over the next decade to gain experience and move up my Community Growth Mountain into the Mid-Career Woods, and even now as I navigate the path toward the Summit, Laura guides me, sending bigger and broader opportunities my way.

What made these opportunities meaningful was the feedback loop we co-created. Through ongoing dialogue and mutual support, Laura and I fostered a sustainable relationship that helped me ascend my Community Growth Mountain but also allowed us to collaborate effectively along each other's journeys.

Laura and I commit to getting together in person twice a year to check in. That brings incredible value to both of us. Why? Because we are both in different places on our respective Growth Mountains, which gives us unique vantage points for seeing opportunities to benefit each other.

We always begin our dinner conversations by asking the other person what's happening. What are you up to? Who are you hanging with that excites you? Why?

Once we share, we offer insights to help the other achieve her goals. In this way, I can bring equal value to Laura. For example, I can leverage my personal connections from my current place on the Growth Mountain and give detailed explanations for why those crowds she noticed last month are gathering on that faraway ridge—a group that dramatically impacts a goal she has this year. Although power dynamics in Mountain Guide relationships exist, value always transcends it. We all learn from one another regardless of where we are presently residing on any given Growth Mountain.

As a result, our relationship blossomed in ways I could never have imagined. Five years later, when a national nonprofit asked Laura to serve as chair, she declined and then suggested that they talk to me. That chair seat ultimately led to the opportunity for me to sit on my first for-profit board—yet another Professional Growth Mountain to navigate.

A few years later, this opportunity catapulted me to new heights on my Professional Mountain because our Growth Mountains are always connected. Always. Because mountains, like people, are never alone. We always exist within the context of a range.

THE MENTOR MOUNTAIN GUIDE WHO SHELTERED ME FROM MY OWN STORMS

One of the toughest things to do on our climb across our Growth Mountain range is to realize—or admit—that we don't know what we don't know. Everyone has knowledge gaps, especially when exploring new lands. That's why we need to build and sustain relationships with our three Mountain Guides.

For me, the realization of the value of a Mentor Mountain Guide came on my journey to become a director on a for-profit board. When the unofficial interview process and vetting began, it became clear to me that this amazing opportunity wasn't just something that "happened" to me. After all, nearly the vast majority of all board seats are filled through relationships that the current board members have.

Between my connections with the Allegheny Conference and my work as Chair of the Pittsburgh chapter of the national initiative called 50/50 Women on Boards, I had a solid strategic network across both my Personal and Community Growth Mountains. While I had nearly fifteen years of nonprofit board experience, I soon found myself at forty years old back down in the Early Career Fields, this time as a for-profit Board Director.

The first Mountain Guide I recruited was a Mentor. And even though this Growth Mountain was slightly different from the others I'd climbed to date, the Wayfinding process and my Wayfinding Compass were the same. I began by identifying my Mountain Guides.

My Board Director Mentor came in the form of a retired executive named Chuck Cohen. Chuck was a seasoned Board

Director to the tune of thirty years. He had written a book on directorship, and he was a university law professor. And fortunately for me, he was also a peer on my new board.

Chuck went out of his way to introduce himself before our first official board meeting. He shared a copy of his book and even took me out to dinner. At our first meeting together, he saved a seat next to him for me. We continued to sit next to one another for the next six years. During my early days, he sometimes passed me notes of support and encouragement, and I always knew he had my back.

Chuck's knowledge and best practices provided me with the understanding that a director contributes not only their knowledge and expertise but also unique opportunities to the company's management team via their own strategic networks, as well as the powerful questions we ask.

As a newbie, my biggest *Aha!* moment with Chuck was at my first board retreat in Florida about six months into navigating the Early Career Fields of this Professional Growth Mountain. I had no idea what was in store in those two days because it's very important for me to be seen as competent, and I often struggle as a "beginner."

I was uneasy and definitely lacked confidence as I headed to this strategic offsite retreat. I knew I wanted to bring value as an expert at this annual meeting. To make matters worse, I was the only outside director who was a woman. So I was off mingling with the men while Kevin was on his own and the other spouses—all women—headed to the shops and spa.

In the three weeks leading up to the March retreat in Florida, the anxiety and anticipation weighed on me like a heavy parka in a scorching desert. In my experience, the Early Career Fields can often feel like an arid, unforgiving landscape where you're wearing the wrong gear, completely out of place, and desperately on the hunt for an oasis of guidance and direction.

Just as a traveler lost in the desert craves water and shelter, early career professionals in every field yearn for mentorship, guidance, and a sense of belonging. The struggle to find your way through this challenging terrain can be both isolating and exhausting, much like the disorienting heat of a desert.

To create even more anxiety, the primary topic of the retreat was human capital and employee engagement, one of the key reasons they recruited me as a Director in the first place. I found myself feeling like I needed to be prepared for anything and everything (there's that self-limiting belief system again). I was certain I would be the center of focus because of my knowledge and understanding of the subject. After all, that's what I was there for, right?

To say I overprepared would be the understatement of the century. I not only read both of Chuck's books and the board retreat PDF cover to cover, drilling deeply down into all the employee data for the company, but I also read two white papers and even took an extra course online from the National Association of Corporate Directors.

As I think about this now, I'm a little embarrassed by my extreme response, but at the time, each step felt necessary so I would be "prepared." I gathered an impressive yet ridiculous collection of questions that I felt would make me look smart and showcase my value. All of this I did from a place of total and complete insecurity, buttressed by my own self-limiting belief systems.

My big mistake, as I later realized, was that through it all, I was working all alone. I certainly didn't ask my Mentor, Chuck, for help. I can see now that it was clearly what I needed to do. In fact, it never even occurred to me to check in with him because I was so stuck in my own head, utterly frozen by my fear and believing that I had to do it alone to prove myself worthy, even to him.

The first morning of the board retreat arrived, and we were immersed in powerful presentations by the management team. I had my questions and responses all queued up, having of course thoroughly researched all the topics beforehand. So I spent the early morning hours laying my "important" questions all out there, intending to show that I totally knew what I was doing and reinforcing that I was a great addition to the board.

When the first break time rolled around and everyone had gotten up to grab a coffee, Chuck leaned over to me, placed his hand on my arm, and asked, "How are you doing?" I answered brightly with a fake smile plastered on my face, "I'm great!"

Then he looked me dead in the eyes, kept his calming hand on my arm, and said, "Christy, you've already earned the right to be here."

At that moment it hit me—*the board retreat wasn't about me.*

As a Mentor Mountain Guide, Chuck served as a mirror, reflecting and reminding me of my own greatness even as my old self-limiting belief systems flared up in my desperation to navigate this new Early Career Field. Even today as I recount this story I can feel how much I loathed being a "beginner" at anything. My go-to reaction to being new was to feel incompetent and so desperately try to perfect, perform, and prove.

Throughout my eight years as a board member, Chuck has

been there beside me as a Mentor Mountain Guide, keeping me steady as I navigated this new Growth Mountain. We all need Mentors like Chuck across *all* our various Growth Mountain Ranges. Right now, I have a powerful Mentor helping me navigate the Early Career Fields as I travel as a beginner on my new Empty Nest Growth Mountain. And while these Mountain Guides likely won't be with us through every journey because we don't need them to be, they will play a key role on new and unfamiliar terrains, helping to shape our Wayfinding Compass and personal evolution journey in powerful ways.

THE COACH MOUNTAIN GUIDE THAT CHANGED MY LIFE

In my time as a Coach and Human Resources leader in the construction industry, I am so grateful for one of the best-of-the-best Coaches I've ever met, a woman named Mary Shippy, CEO of Align Leadership. Mary was my Coach when I was the Vice President of Human Resources in the construction industry. Our connection was so close that ultimately I became her business partner.

After my seven years as an internal Coach, in 2013 I went back out to the consulting world. Instead of seeing other Coaches as competition as I did when I was a solopreneur at Red Zebra, I accepted an offer from Mary to incubate EDGE Leadership under her company's successful global coaching umbrella. And that's how Mary became one of the most powerful Coach Mountain Guides in my life.

Partnering with Mary was an intentional and powerful strategy. Not only did I receive an instant and accessible Coach, but I also was able to position my Third Place model to Fortune 500 companies. With Mary and her company beside me, I now was perceived to be bigger than on my own. I opened the East Coast office of Align and focused on trademarking the model I had been beta testing in my spare time with EMPOWER, the CoT, and SWSG. I named it the PEER Technology Framework and embarked on growing my group coaching business with Mary's help.

Equally important to the business strategy was my personal development. Mary was always more than my business partner and to this day remains a dear friend. A powerful Coach, Mary could toggle between advice-giving roles of mentorship and walking beside me as a Coach Mountain Guide in my Mountain trek, asking questions and helping me generate my own solutions to the challenges that inevitably would arise along the journey.

When I stopped beside a large clearing in the Mid-Career Woods, instead of rushing me along, she'd ask, "What interests you about staying here? Why do you think so?"

Mary was brilliant at keeping her advice to herself unless I specifically asked for her mentorship, and she always challenged me to let go of my self-limiting beliefs. She encouraged me to leverage my youth as a differentiator, not a detractor, as we launched the East Coast Office of Align Leadership that we built together, offering group coaching and creating mentoring and coaching circles inside companies and across industries.

Thanks to Mary's coaching, I began reprogramming my self-limiting belief that my youth was a negative, an outdated perspective left over from my first foray into navigating the Entrepreneurship Growth Mountain. I began instead to say to organizations, "You want to hire a Coach that looks like the people being coached. That's me. Hire a Millennial to build and deliver your high-potential young leader programs!"

While this mindset shift may seem small, the impact was dramatic. In fact, when I changed my belief system about selling, it led to crazy success with group coaching, expanding Align's total revenue fivefold in the first five years.

I am forever indebted to Mary as my Coach Mountain Guide in my business and life. She was the guiding star on my Wayfinding journey, illuminating the path long before I saw it myself. Without her, my Wayfinding Compass for navigating life's challenges would not be complete.

As we cross the intricate landscapes of our Professional and Personal Growth Mountains, it's crucial to remember that the journey is seldom a straight path. Seasoned sailors understand that true north is never held in a straight line on the open sea since conditions change moment by moment. Similarly, in leadership and life, our personal evolution is continuously evolving.

9

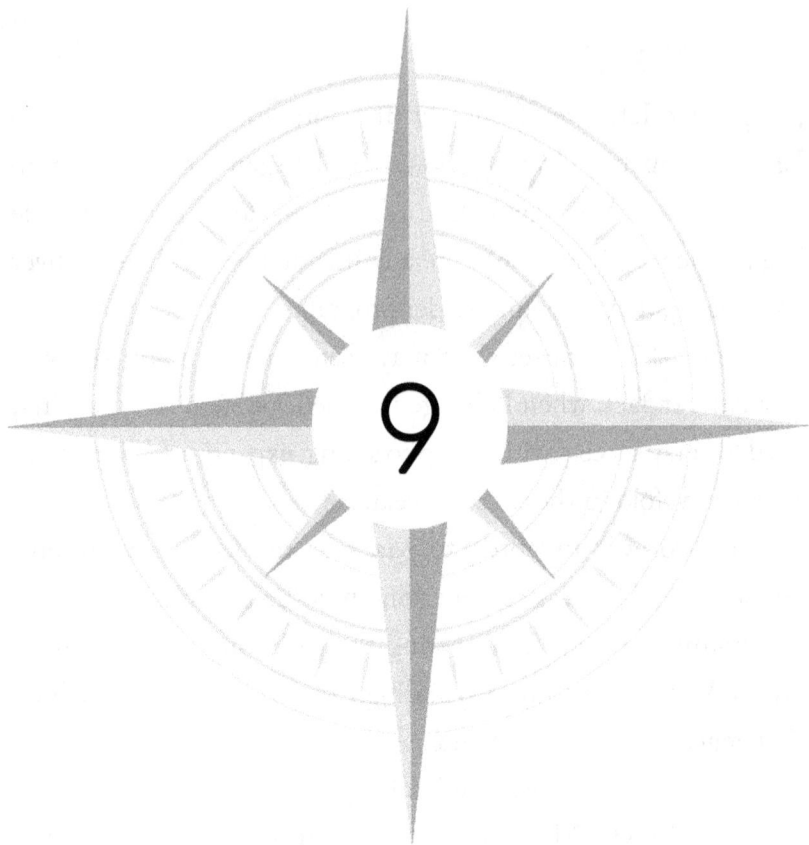

YOU HAVE YOUR COMPASS AND YOUR MOUNTAIN GUIDES

Now What?

Just as no two Wayfinding journeys are identical, neither are the ascents and traversals of our unique Growth Mountains, whether personal or professional. Each of us leaves behind a distinct travel route, forging our own unique path as we navigate the terrain. Similarly, the individuals we encounter on our

Wayfinding journey are as diverse and distinct as the landscapes we explore.

The most beautiful part of our journeys is the opportunity to pay it forward. While we depend on both our peers and our Mountain Guides to help us along the way, others will also need us and our knowledge, experience, and perspective to serve in those same roles. A woman named Keisha Pendleton is a beautiful example of the power of paying it forward to others in her peer cohort group.

Keisha heard about the power of our Third Places at EDGE Leadership and decided to take part in one of our open enrollment cohorts in 2017 while working at Carlow University in Pittsburgh as a Project Manager. From the onset, Keisha gave herself permission to engage in very deep conversations with her peers. She felt the energy was electrifying. Everyone gave themselves permission to become vulnerable and opened up to one another as we co-created their peer mentoring and group coaching cohort and charted a course toward their Individual EDGE Outcomes as a peer group (creating their own unique Wayfinding Compass, of course).

As a Black woman, Keisha's EDGE Outcome was to gain confidence and effectively network in circles that didn't always look like her. When I met Keisha, I saw the personal power within her, but I'm not so sure she did. She readily admitted that she lacked confidence within herself, perhaps because, as she said at the time, she had been Wayfinding through a rough patch in her life, both personally and professionally.

She came to EDGE Leadership to learn and connect with peer Mentors and Coaches and chart a course to identify the Mountain Guides she needed to navigate her Personal and

Professional Growth Mountains. But she had no idea she would end up contributing just as much, if not more, than she received. Over the course of the nine-month development program, Keisha was able to give back and powerfully mentor and coach the other folks in the cohort who were currently Wayfinding themselves through their careers and personal transformations.

As their Wayfinding skill level and desire for Self-Awareness, Self-Alignment, Self-Trust, and Self-Worth increased, Keisha's EDGE cohort began to practice deeper vulnerability in decision-making, powerfully shifting the ways they processed life overall and each fine-tuning their own Wayfinding Compass to navigate the uncharted territory ahead on their Growth Mountains. Listening to everyone tell their stories and tapping into the vulnerability levels helped Keisha take a hard look at her Wayfinding Compass to determine how she was interpreting her role in the world and, most importantly, how and where she wanted to shift it.

As a result of the increased Self-Alignment and Self-Trust, Keisha learned firsthand that the power of a Third Place holding each other accountable, asking for support, and sharing successes is life-changing. She truly benefited from having easy and consistent access to a cohort of peer Coaches serving as accountability partners for her, knowing that someone else was going to check up on her personal and professional goals each month. This new, elevated level of vulnerable and consistent peer support helped Keisha powerfully shift her priorities on her Personal Growth Mountain. For example, if she wanted to exercise but didn't feel as though she had the time, her peers would consistently follow up and remind her of her own priorities to herself and hold her accountable to build Self-Trust.

Keisha was able to develop the confidence and Self-Worth she needed, thanks to her Third Place. After completing the EDGE peer mentoring and group coaching experience, as she would proudly tell you today, she became a new woman. Participating in EDGE provided Keisha with an enormous number of resources and gave her the opportunity to connect with many great leaders, both as her peers and a guest mentor who ultimately became an Advocate Mountain Guide in her career.

Within five months of graduating from EDGE, Keisha was promoted to a position she had wanted for some time. She realized that what she was missing before was having consistent Self-Trust that no matter what life brought her, she could navigate it. And if she didn't find the answers within herself, she had a powerful group of peers she could go to for resources, ideas, and support. Realizing that she was not alone also increased her confidence and Self-Worth. Through calibrating her Wayfinding Compass, Keisha found her voice and claimed and truly owned her seat at the table.

Not surprisingly, two years later, in 2019, Keisha was promoted again, and then she boldly relocated to a new industry and a new state. Although she is the only person of color on her project, she recently shared with me that she is loving life on this New Growth Mountain. She also proudly told me that she was not only able to implement all the Wayfinding tools acquired through EDGE but also maintain relationships with the other women in her peer cohort years later.

Keisha is a powerful example of the PEER Technology Framework and Third Spaces in action—both contributing to and being contributed by her fellow cohort members as peer Mentors,

Advocates, and Coaches. Not only did Keisha find accountability partners and a wealth of mentorship opportunities within her group coaching experience, but she also got to engage with executives as guest Mentors.

These leaders brought vertical knowledge transfer to the cohort of peers and created the space for Advocate and Mentor Mountain Guides to take root. Her fellow EDGE cohort members also had an enormous collection of connections with many great leaders inside their strategic networks. Keisha now found that she had access to a vast mountain range of people and possibilities. And in exchange, Keisha equally shared access to her personal and professional connections that best served her peers on their Growth Mountain journeys. The connections and impact increase to this day.

BUILDING AND SUSTAINING YOUR
THIRD PLACE

Once you've added a new Mountain Guide to your Compass or joined a Peer Mentoring circle, nurturing these connections becomes an integral part of your journey. To truly embrace the essence of your Compass of Mountain Guides, it's crucial to approach these relationships with a transformational mindset rather than a transactional one. In the realm of personal evolution, authenticity resonates deeply. We were never meant to live or Wayfind alone, and we thrive in the community of our Third Place. We flourish on mutual understanding and strength of relationships where we contribute and gain in equal measure.

While embracing a transformational approach, it's equally vital to maintain a strategic perspective to ensure the relationship remains mutually beneficial. Just as my experience with Laura, my Advocate Mountain Guide, demonstrated, strategically aligning your interactions can help both you and your Mountain Guide achieve your respective goals while fostering a lasting and enriching connection across a Third Place.

To create authentic connection across your Third Place, you will want to develop an environment of shared safety and vulnerability. It's difficult to overestimate the importance of vulnerability when it comes to achieving higher levels of personal and professional success, especially when it comes to peer mentoring. It all starts with the courage to take a risk and share your story. Maintaining our Third Place means modeling vulnerability across the Wayfinding Compass of Self-Awareness, Self-Alignment, Self-Trust, and Self-Worth. You have to continue to circle back to each aspect as needed and let your peers accompany you on your journey, just as you in turn do the same for them. We give *and* receive.

When what is shared gets validated and met with empathy from others, it promotes an environment of support and encouragement. That is why the Third Place is so critical. When people co-create a place where it is safe to talk openly and honestly, human potential can really take off across any Growth Mountain Range, personal or professional. It is this vulnerability that fosters the intimacy needed to build dynamic, connecting, and collaborative relationships.

Openly sharing with others can fail quite spectacularly if we do not purposefully create a brave, intentional space for success. That's because in order to speak, people *must* feel empowered to take what we perceive as a huge risk—the risk of being judged.

How do we overcome the barriers that can sometimes keep us from opening up? As we have discussed, vulnerability often feels scary, revealing, and exposing. Talking about yourself can feel fraught with peril, especially with (gulp) work colleagues if you choose to build your Third Place in the workplace like we do here at EDGE Leadership, and it actually can be if you don't know what you're doing. But without vulnerability, human potential is limited. In order to improve at anything, we have to be able to clearly see where we are and admit we need help.

When we witness someone embrace Wayfinding and share something significant from their journey, we cannot help but feel a profound connection to the shared human experience. *Me too*, our hearts say. *Me too*. And while we think we most fear the judgment of others, in reality, *no one* judges us more harshly than we judge ourselves. As adults, we have become so used to hearing that harsh judgment in our own heads and hearts that we just assume others will do the same or worse, so we self-protect. And when we do, we miss the opportunity to build Self-Trust.

Vulnerability begets vulnerability. When we choose to show up as our imperfect selves, to set aside our self-limiting beliefs that keep us small and stuck, we unconsciously give permission to our peers to do the same. Over the last few decades of my work as a leadership and now reinvention coach, one by one, each person is inspired by the Wayfinders who journeyed before them. Through vulnerability, everyone becomes more and more comfortable sharing their personal and professional journeys. We can truly let ourselves be seen by contributing in a way that is transparent with one another and models the absence of judgment.

Strategic Mountain Guide relationships play a pivotal role in personal and professional growth, and I encourage you to layer them into the creation of your Third Place as well. They offer the perspective, resources, and means to expand, impact, and advance not only careers but our fulfillment on our Personal Growth Mountain as well. These relationships become a network that serves as the scaffolding for achieving our Wayfinding goals and living a more fulfilled and joyful life.[14]

While we may tend toward networks and Peer Mentoring groups with more similarities than differences, Wayfinding intensifies when we embrace diversity of ideas, inputs, and resources. There is power to be found in connections with people in our Third Places whose strengths fill our gaps.

I've found in my Wayfinding journey that for a Strategic Network to be impactful, it must embody certain qualities. It should be broad and connect with a diverse range of people. It should be connective, bridging folks that may not naturally intersect. And most importantly, it should be dynamic—responsive and adaptive, growing in tandem with personal development.

Building a Third Place takes intentionality and drive. Research shows it can be especially difficult for women and people of color who are often in the minority in many corporate environments. The best way to cultivate these connections starts with engaging in activities both inside and outside the organization, leveraging existing connections, and actively focusing on the unique value you bring to the peer network. Prioritizing and actively investing in a select few activities such as a monthly meeting together or informal weekly meet-ups will ensure that your Third Place not only supports your group's current endeavors but also evolves alongside their personal and professional growth as they do.

PREPARING FOR YOUR SUMMIT

Every time we navigate a Growth Mountain, we have the opportunity to give to and receive across our Third Place. We all benefit from recognizing the importance of human connection and leaning into it, no matter where we are in our lives. Sometimes we need folks to serve in the roles of Mentor, Advocate, and Coach for us in our own personal evolution as we Wayfind across our Growth Mountains at work and at home. And sometimes we serve in those roles for others. As peers, we are always coming alongside those in our Third Places to support, challenge, invite, share, and love. An authentic Third Place is both/and not either/or. As I have said many times in this book, it is found in the tension between self *and* others, individual *and* collective, micro *and* macro.

Since I launched EDGE Leadership in 2013, I've had a goal to serve as an Advocate for a minimum of five of my EDGE group coaching graduates, helping them get on nonprofit boards every year. This adds value, I hope, not only for the individuals but also for the great nonprofits looking for new, talented board members. Double impact.

I am also hard at work annually amplifying the impact and the influence I have as a Mentor. I actively mentor at least three women of color entrepreneurs each year who want to start or scale their businesses as a way to continue to be intentional about supporting women entrepreneurs. As I do, they in turn become Mentors to me as I see firsthand the additional barriers and obstacles women of color face that white women who look like me do not. These relationships have not only increased my knowledge in how I can show up in more impactful ways to our diverse cohort members but have also taught me so much about empathy, compassion, strength, and power.

In this way, we Mountain Guide one another. Although I am a professional Coach, I will never stop looking for people to fill these key roles in my life, including working with great Coaches every chance I get. For over twenty years, I have always hired my own Coach each year so I can put myself in the intentional and uncomfortable developmental space of being a beginner. Not only does doing so allow me to walk authentically and continue my own personal evolution process, but I believe that always being coached makes me a better Coach too. We become fulfilled and wholehearted people, not just leaders, when we allow ourselves to stay in that tension of being both learners *and* teachers.

On my Personal Growth Mountain, I am currently being mentored by a few amazing empty nesters. Eli is turning twenty-two this summer and headed into his senior year in college. Before I know it, he will be out of school and building his life as a full-fledged adult. And I know that I want to continue to be a support to him personally and professionally, and hopefully also to his life partner and family if he chooses to Wayfind in that direction.

A Mentor who was so precious to me and helped me launch EDGE was M. J. Tocci, the founder of the Heinz Negotiation Academy for Women at Carnegie Mellon University. I will never forget when she told me more than a decade ago something that perfectly articulates this point. She said, "For every path we walk through in life, we have a responsibility to grab the hands of ten people and bring them with us. And then prop the damn door open for 10,000 more."

I love that image so much. What if we can do that right now? Let's lock arms together as peers because no matter where we are Wayfinding next on our own Growth Mountains, we know we are no longer traveling alone. And if you bring ten, and I bring ten, and *they* bring ten, we will reach 10,000 before we know it.

AFTERWORD
Mapmaking: It's Your Time to Climb

begin again. Not because I failed but because I am worth re-
turning to.

Wayfinding is an invitation to step outside the boundaries of
your life and mindset as you know it and go on a brave pilgrimage
to the unknown. There are no maps in this territory, no marked
paths, no road signs, no GPS. The time to embark on your personal
evolution is here. I urge you to not linger in the port as distant
shores are calling. And remember that we were never meant to
travel alone.

Personal evolution is not a solitary act. It is communal. When
we become aware of who we are and what we want, challenging
our belief systems and shifting how we choose to show up to
those we most love, to the world, and most of all to ourselves, we
unconsciously give permission to others to do the same. This, my
friends, is how we change the world.

By changing ourselves.

Calibrating the Wayfinding Compass that already lives deep
inside our Belly is a journey, not a destination. It is never-ending,
continuous.

And isn't it kind of a relief to realize it's not supposed to end, that no amount of "fixing" yourself will ever make you whole? The most true *you* is already whole. It can't be broken.

It has never *been* broken.

Wholeness is not something you achieve; it is something you remember. This work is not personal mastery. After all, there is no such thing as mastering our life. Wayfinding is an evolution. And wherever you find yourself on your Wayfinding Compass right now, today—Self-Awareness, Self-Alignment, Self-Trust, or Self-Worth—you can *always* begin again.

I hope I effectively, although quite imperfectly, opened this conversation with you. Peer Mentoring, Community, the power of a Third Place, whatever you choose to call it, is as elegantly simple as it is effective. And it is sustainable because it is based on leveraging best practices of the collective to ignite the individual. As we Wayfind together, we each take turns giving and receiving. Sometimes we are the ones finding inspiration, and other times we ignite it in others.

In both cases, I believe this is the core of what we need so desperately in our world today—Connection. Belonging. Empathy. Being Seen.

And being Heard.

My friends, it is okay to be afraid of what comes next as long as we choose to take action anyway! Courage is not the absence of fear. It is acknowledging our fear and doing it anyway. Saying it anyway. Leaping anyway.

When we do, we can clearly see that fear is a liar.

Because we can be both *brave* and *afraid* at exactly the same time.

It does not matter that you do not know where you are headed just yet. Simply start where you are. Trust yourself. If you do, when the next step arrives, you will know how to take it.

As you evolve, you will discover that Wayfinding is less about your place in the world and more about your place inside yourself.

And when you find *you* again—don't let yourself go.

ENDNOTES

1   You can read more about my Vulnerability Model, including the Head, Heart, and Belly, in my book The PEER Revolution: Group Coaching That Ignites the Power of People.

2   Najwa Zebian, Welcome Home: A Guide to Building a Home for Your Soul (Harmony Books, 2021), 108.

3   Richard C. Schwartz, "No Bad Parts," IFS Institute, n.d., https://ifs-institute.com/nobadparts.

4   Brené Brown, "Own Our History. Change Our Story," Brené Brown, https://brenebrown.com/articles/2015/06/18/own-our-history-change-the-story, June 18, 2015.

5   Amy C. Edmondson, The Fearless Organization: Creating Psychological Safety in the Workplace for Learning, Innovation, and Growth (Wiley, 2018).

6   "Understanding Unconscious Bias," NPR, July 15, 2020, https://www.npr.org/2020/07/14/891140598/understanding-unconscious-bias.

7   John Delony, Redefining Anxiety: What It Is, What It's Not, and How to Get Your Life Back (Ramsey Press, 2020).

8   Emily Nagoski and Amelia Nagoski, Burnout: The Secret to Unlocking the Stress Cycle (Ballantine Books, 2019), 62.

9   Jim Loehr and Tony Schwartz, "The Making of a Corporate Athlete," Harvard Business Review, January 2001, https://hbr.org/2001/01/the-making-of-a-corporate-athlete.

10 Cory Muscara, "Wholeness," Practicing Human, November 10, 2022, https://practicinghuman.buzzsprout.com/597910/episodes/11667904-wholeness.

11 Caroline Myss, Anatomy of the Spirit: The Seven Stages of Power and Healing (Harmony Books, 2017), 273.

12 Herminia Ibarra, "Why Strategic Networks Are Important for Women and How to Build Them," September 27, 2017, https://herminiaibarra. com/why-strategic-networks-are-important-for-women-and-how-to-build-them/.

13 Herminia Ibarra, Working Identity: Unconventional Strategies for Reinventing Your Career (Boston: Harvard Business School Press, 2003).

14 Check out Chapter 9, Relevant Content, in The PEER Revolution for best practices on how to find, enroll, and engage these Mountain Guides well.

www.ingramcontent.com/pod-product-compliance
Lightning Source LLC
Chambersburg PA
CBHW071232210326
41597CB00016B/2019